BOOK OF NURSERY AND MOTHER GOOSE RHYMES

Marguerite de Angeli's

BOOK OF NURSERY

AND

MOTHER GOOSE

RHYMES

Doubleday

NEW YORK LONDON TORONTO SYDNEY AUCKLAND

Smiling girls, rosy boys,
Come and buy my little toys—
Monkeys made of gingerbread,
And sugar-horses painted red.

Published by Doubleday, a division of
Bantam Doubleday Dell Publishing Group, Inc.,
666 Fifth Avenue, New York, New York 10103.

Doubleday and the portrayal of an anchor with a dolphin
are trademarks of Doubleday, a division of
Bantam Doubleday Dell Publishing Group, Inc.

Copyright, 1953, 1954, by Marguerite de Angeli
Library of Congress Catalog Card Number 54–9838
Lithographed in the U. S. A.
Designed by Alma Reese Cardi
All Rights Reserved

ISBN: 0-385-07232-5 TRADE
ISBN: 0-385-15291 PAPERBACK
26   28   30   32   33   31   29   27

OG

1996

To our precious Elizabeth on your first Easter,

All our love and hugs and kisses,

Grampy and Grammy

THIS BOOK
IS DEDICATED
TO ALL CHILDREN
EVERYWHERE
AND
ALWAYS
M. DE A.

FOREWORD

When I think of the nursery rhymes and my first memory of them, I remember my mother, sitting in a low rocker, singing during a thunderstorm. What she was singing is not clear. It could have been "Sing a Song of Sixpence," "Rock-a-bye Baby," or any one of the familiar rhymes, or all of them, for there were many rockings and many comfortings. Later, when my younger brothers came along, I often sat in my mother's place and sang to them, choosing my own favorites and making up the tunes as I went. In those days we sang and rocked the children to sleep, and felt their dear heaviness when they finally gave up the fight to keep awake.

Still later, when I had been married and we had children of our own, the habit of singing the nursery rhymes was continued, and now that we have grandchildren, it goes on. They still listen as long as words continue, and at the pause for breath say, "Do it again."

Sometimes, instead of my mother's voice, it is my English grandfather's voice that I hear when I think of "Please to remember the fifth of November" and Guy Fawkes' Day, or it is my father's voice saying, "Theophilus Thistle, the successful thistle sifter."

When my husband and I went to England a few years ago, those early mental images came alive. And now the flowery fields and blossoming hedgerows, the stone walls and castles, the cobblestone streets have all crept into the pictures for the nursery rhymes. A twelfth-century bridge I sketched turned up in the painting for "Hark, Hark, the Dogs do bark"; the oven in the kitchen at Hampton Court I remembered when I drew the Queen of Hearts. In my mind Wee Willie Winkie has always run down a narrow cobbled street and around a corner as I pictured him, and I saw many streets where he belonged. The chalky cliffs with the cap of green that are in "I saw three ships a-sailing" were the cliffs of Dover that we saw when we crossed the Channel.

In the pictures of children, our own children are represented, of course, but new types have come forth that resemble our grandchildren. I was surprised to find, after it was finished, that in "Bless the Master of This House" I had pictured my own brothers and sister, my mother and father, in our right age relation, sitting around the table. Though it was unconscious, perhaps it was natural, because all the time I was so happily painting I had been thinking how much we used to enjoy the "current" baby in his high chair and how we all loved Christmas. No doubt Bob Cratchitt's family came into my mind too, and that accounts for the period of the costume.

Saying or singing the rhymes seems always to open a long corridor in my mind through which I see generations of mothers going about their needful work, the children at their heels or in their laps enchanted by the rhythmic sound of words; words that are sometimes pure nonsense, sometimes full of age-old wisdom, or seeming to have lost their meaning because of time and custom past. One of the favorites in our family has been "One misty, moisty morning," partly because we often have that kind of morning in Philadelphia, but mostly because it was our daughter Nina's favorite when she could barely say it, and her way of saying it lent it charm. Not long ago, when I came upon an article in the *National Geographic* about the Jutland man so well preserved in the peatland since the seventh century, still wearing his leather cap with a strap beneath his chin, I had the uncanny feeling that he was the very man of the rhyme. After all, that particular rhyme is thought to be one of the most ancient, going back hundreds and hundreds of years, long before there were books of rhymes and pictures.

I have loved doing the book.

Marguerite de Angeli

BOOK OF NURSERY AND MOTHER GOOSE RHYMES

Peter, Peter, pumpkin eater,
Had a wife and couldn't keep her;
He put her in a pumpkin shell
And there he kept her very well.

Peter, Peter, pumpkin eater,
Had another, and didn't love her;
Peter learned to read and spell,
And then he loved her very well.

Three wise men of Gotham,
They went to sea in a bowl,
And if the bowl had been stronger
My song had been longer.

Little Jack Horner
Sat in the corner,
Eating a Christmas pie;
He put in his thumb,
And pulled out a plum,
And said, What a good boy am I!

Wee Willie Winkie runs through the town,
Upstairs and downstairs in his nightgown,
Rapping at the window, crying through the lock,
"Are the children in their beds, for now it's eight o'clock?"

The dove says, Coo, coo, what shall I do?
I can scarce maintain two.
Pooh, pooh, says the wren, I have ten,
And keep them all like gentlemen.

Handy spandy, Jack-a-Dandy,
Loves plum cake and sugar candy;
He bought some at a grocer's shop,
And out he came, hop, hop, hop, hop.

Needles and pins, needles and pins,
When a man marries his trouble begins.

One I love, two I love,
 Three I love, I say,
Four I love with all my heart,
 Five I cast away;
Six he loves, seven she loves, eight they both love,
 Nine he comes, ten he tarries,
Eleven he courts, twelve he marries.

I had a little hobby horse
And it was dapple gray,
Its head was made of pea-straw,
Its tail was made of hay.

I sold him to an old woman
For a copper groat,
And I'll not sing my song again
Without a new coat.

Pussy cat Mole jumped over a coal
And in her best petticoat burnt a great hole.
Poor pussy's weeping, she'll have no more milk
Until her best petticoat's mended with silk.

Long legs, crooked thighs,
Little head and no eyes.

                ] *Tongs*

Black we are, but much admired;
Men seek for us till they are tired.
We tire the horse, but comfort man:
Tell me this riddle if you can.

        ] *Coals*

Little Miss Muffet
Sat on a tuffet,
Eating her curds and whey;
There came a big spider,
Who sat down beside her
And frightened Miss Muffet away.

13

There was a piper had a cow,
  And he had nought to give her.
He pulled out his pipes and played her a tune,
  And bade the cow consider.

  The cow considered very well
    And gave the piper a penny,
  And bade him play the other tune,
    "Corn rigs are bonny."

Charlie Warlie had a cow,
Black and white about the brow;
Open the gate and let her through,
Charlie Warlie's old cow.

There was a little man, and he had a little gun,
    And his bullets were made of lead, lead, lead;
He went to the brook, and shot a little duck,
    Right through the middle of the head, head, head.

    He carried it home to his old wife Joan,
        And bade her a fire for to make, make, make,
    To roast the little duck he had shot in the brook,
        And he'd go and fetch her the drake, drake, drake.

        The drake was swimming, with his curly tail,
          The little man made it his mark, mark, mark;
        But he let off his gun, and he fired too soon,
          And the drake flew away with a quack, quack quack.

      Little drops of water,
        Little grains of sand,
      Make the mighty ocean,
        And the pleasant land.

Little ships must keep the shore;
Larger ships may venture more.

Curly locks, Curly locks,
    Wilt thou be mine?
Thou shalt not wash dishes
    Nor yet feed the swine,
But sit on a cushion
    And sew a fine seam,
And feed upon strawberries,
    Sugar and cream.

      Here am I,
      Little Jumping Joan;
      When nobody's with me
      I'm all alone.

My father left me three acres of land,
   Sing ivy, sing ivy;
My father left me three acres of land,
   Sing holly, go whistle and ivy!

I ploughed it with a ram's horn,
   Sing ivy, sing ivy;
And sowed it all over with one pepper corn,
   Sing holly, go whistle and ivy!

I harrowed it with a bramble bush,
   Sing ivy, sing ivy;
And reaped it with my little penknife,
   Sing holly, go whistle and ivy!

I got the mice to carry it to the barn,
   Sing ivy, sing ivy;
And thrashed it with a goose's quill,
   Sing holly, go whistle and ivy!

I got the cat to carry it to the mill,
   Sing ivy, sing ivy;
The miller he swore he would have her paw,
And the cat she swore she would scratch his face,
   Sing holly, go whistle and ivy!

Rosemary green, and lavender blue,
Thyme and sweet marjoram, hyssop and rue.

Lavender's blue, diddle, diddle,
   Lavender's green;
When I am king, diddle, diddle,
   You shall be queen.

One misty, moisty, morning,
When cloudy was the weather,
I chanced to meet an old man
Clothed all in leather;
Clothed all in leather,
With a strap beneath his chin.
How do you do, and how do you do,
And how do you do again?

Tommy Trot, a man of law,
Sold his bed and lay upon straw;
Sold the straw and slept on grass,
To buy his wife a looking-glass.

The girl in the lane, that couldn't speak plain,
Cried, "Gobble, gobble, gobble."
The man on the hill, that couldn't stand still,
Went hobble, hobble, hobble.

This is the house that Jack built.

This is the malt
That lay in the house that Jack built.

This is the rat,
That ate the malt
That lay in the house that Jack built.

This is the cat,
That killed the rat,
That ate the malt
That lay in the house that Jack built.

This is the dog,
That worried the cat,
That killed the rat,
That ate the malt
That lay in the house that Jack built.

This is the cow with the crumpled horn,
That tossed the dog,
That worried the cat,
That killed the rat,
That ate the malt
That lay in the house that Jack built.

This is the maiden all forlorn,
That milked the cow with the crumpled horn,
That tossed the dog,
That worried the cat,
That killed the rat,
That ate the malt
That lay in the house that Jack built.

This is the man all tattered and torn,
That kissed the maiden all forlorn,
That milked the cow with the crumpled horn,
That tossed the dog,
That worried the cat,
That killed the rat,
That ate the malt
That lay in the house that Jack built.

This is the priest all shaven and shorn,
That married the man all tattered and torn,
That kissed the maiden all forlorn,
That milked the cow with the crumpled horn,
That tossed the dog,
That worried the cat,
That killed the rat,
That ate the malt
That lay in the house that Jack built.

This is the cock that crowed in the morn,
That waked the priest all shaven and shorn,
That married the man all tattered and torn,
That kissed the maiden all forlorn,
That milked the cow with the crumpled horn,
That tossed the dog,
That worried the cat,
That killed the rat,
That ate the malt
That lay in the house that Jack built.

This is the farmer sowing his corn,
That kept the cock that crowed in the morn,
That waked the priest all shaven and shorn,
That married the man all tattered and torn,
That kissed the maiden all forlorn,
That milked the cow with the crumpled horn,
That tossed the dog,
That worried the cat,
That killed the rat,
That ate the malt
That lay in the house that Jack built.

Humpty Dumpty sat on a wall,
Humpty Dumpty had a great fall.
    All the king's horses,
    And all the king's men,
Couldn't put Humpty together again.

For every evil under the sun,
There is a remedy, or there is none.
If there be one, try and find it;
If there be none, never mind it.

Flour of England, fruit of Spain,
Met together in a shower of rain,
Put in a bag and tied round with a string,
If you'll tell me this riddle, I'll give you a ring.

                ] *A plum pudding*

There was an old woman, and what do you think?
She lived upon nothing but victuals and drink:
Victuals and drink were the chief of her diet,
And yet this old woman could never keep quiet. 21

A sunshiny shower
Won't last half an hour.

Rain, rain, go away,
Come again another day.

Friday night's dream
On the Saturday told,
Is sure to come true,
Be it ever so old.

Girls and boys come out to play,
The moon doth shine as bright as day.
Leave your supper and leave your sleep,
And come with your playfellows into the street.
Come with a whoop, come with a call,
Come with a good will or not at all.
Up the ladder and down the wall,
A halfpenny roll will serve us all;
You find milk, and I'll find flour,
And we'll have a pudding in half an hour.

London Bridge is broken down,
  Broken down, broken down,
London Bridge is broken down,
  My fair lady.

Build it up with wood and clay,
  Wood and clay, wood and clay,
Build it up with wood and clay,
  My fair lady.

Wood and clay will wash away,
  Wash away, wash away,
Wood and clay will wash away,
  My fair lady.

Build it up with bricks and mortar,
  Bricks and mortar, bricks and mortar,
Build it up with bricks and mortar,
  My fair lady.

Bricks and mortar will not stay,
  Will not stay, will not stay,
Bricks and mortar will not stay,
  My fair lady.

    Build it up with iron and steel,
      Iron and steel, iron and steel,
    Build it up with iron and steel,
      My fair lady.

        Iron and steel will bend and bow,
          Bend and bow, bend and bow,
        Iron and steel will bend and bow,
          My fair lady.

            Build it up with silver and gold,
              Silver and gold, silver and gold,
            Build it up with silver and gold,
              My fair lady.

      Silver and gold will be stolen away,
        Stolen away, stolen away,
      Silver and gold will be stolen away,
        My fair lady.

                Set a man to watch all night,
                  Watch all night, watch all night,
                Set a man to watch all night,
                  My fair lady.

Solomon Grundy,
Born on a Monday,
Christened on Tuesday,
Married on Wednesday,
Took ill on Thursday,
Worse on Friday,
Died on Saturday,
Buried on Sunday.
This is the end
Of Solomon Grundy.

There was a little boy and a little girl,
    Lived in an alley;
Says the little boy to the little girl,
    Shall I, oh, shall I?

                    Says the little girl to the little boy,
                        What shall we do?
                    Says the little boy to the little girl,
                        I will kiss you!

Leg over leg,
    As the dog went to Dover,
When he came to a stile,
    Jump he went over.

Come, let's to bed,
Says Sleepy-head;
Tarry a while, says Slow;
Put on the pot,
Says Greedy-gut,
We'll sup before we go.

The miller he grinds his corn, his corn;
The miller he grinds his corn, his corn;
The little Boy Blue comes winding his horn,
With a hop, skip, and a jump.

The carter he whistles aside his team;
The carter he whistles aside his team;
And Dolly comes tripping with the nice clouted cream,
With a hop, skip, and a jump.

The nightingale sings when we're at rest;
The nightingale sings when we're at rest;
The little bird climbs the tree for his nest,
With a hop, skip, and a jump.

The damsels are churning for curds and whey;
The damsels are churning for curds and whey;
The lads in the fields are making the hay,
With a hop, skip, and a jump.

27

Twelve pears hanging high,
Twelve knights riding by;
Each knight took a pear,
And yet left eleven there.

St Swithin's Day if thou dost rain,
For forty days it will remain;
St Swithin's Day if thou be fair,
For forty days 'twill rain na mair.

Little Bo-peep has lost her sheep,
    And can't tell where to find them;
Leave them alone, and they'll come home,
    And bring their tails behind them.

Little Bo-peep fell fast asleep,
    And dreamt she heard them bleating;
But when she awoke, she found it a joke,
    For they were still all fleeting.

Then up she took her little crook,
    Determined for to find them;
She found them indeed, but it made her heart bleed,
    For they'd left their tails behind them.

It happened one day, as Bo-peep did stray
    Into a meadow hard by,
There she espied their tails side by side,
    All hung on a tree to dry.

She heaved a sigh, and wiped her eye,
    And over the hillocks went rambling,
And tried what she could, as a shepherdess should,
    To tack again each to its lambkin.

A little cock sparrow sat on a green tree,
And he chirruped, he chirruped, so merry was he.
A naughty boy came with his wee bow and arrow,
Says he, "I will shoot this little cock sparrow;
His body will make me a nice little stew,
And his giblets will make me a little pie too."

"Oh, no," said the sparrow, "I won't make a stew,"
So he clapped his wings and away he flew.

Daffy-Down-Dilly has come up to town,
In a yellow petticoat, and a green gown.

Peter White will ne'er go right;
Would you know the reason why?
He follows his nose wherever he goes,
And that stands all awry.

I had a little moppet,
I kept it in my pocket
And fed it on corn and hay;
Then came a proud beggar
And said he would wed her,
And stole my little moppet away.

Old Mother Twitchett had but one eye,
And a long tail, which she let fly;
And everytime she went over a gap,
She left a bit of her tail in a trap.

]*A needle and thread*

Elizabeth, Elspeth, Betsy and Bess,
They all went together to seek a bird's nest;
They found a bird's nest with five eggs in,
They all took one, and left four in.

Hush, baby, my doll, I pray you don't cry,
And I'll give you some bread and some milk by and by;
Or, perhaps, you like custard, or, maybe, a tart—
Then to either you're welcome, with all my whole heart.

A duck and a drake,
A nice barley cake,
With a penny to pay the old baker;
A hop and a scotch
Is another notch,
Slitherum, slatherum, take her.

It was on a merry time
   When Jenny Wren was young,
So neatly as she danced,
   And so sweetly as she sung.

Robin Redbreast lost his heart,
   He was a gallant bird;
He doffed his hat to Jenny,
   And thus to her he said:

"My dearest Jenny Wren,
   If you will but be mine,
You shall dine on cherry pie,
   And drink nice currant wine;

"I'll dress you like a goldfinch,
   Or like a peacock gay;
So if you'll have me, Jenny,
   Let us appoint the day."

Jenny blushed behind her fan,
   And thus declared her mind:
"Then let it be to-morrow, Bob,
   I take your offer kind;

"Cherry pie is very good,
   So is currant wine;
But I'll wear my russet gown,
   And never dress too fine."

Robin rose up early
   At the break of day,
He flew to Jenny Wren's house,
   To sing a roundelay.

He sang of Robin's love
   For little Jenny Wren,
And when he came unto the end,
   Then he began again.

The birds were asked to dine;
   Not Jenny's friends alone,
But every pretty songster
   That had Cock Robin known.

They had a cherry pie,
   Besides some currant wine;
And every guest brought something,
   That sumptuous they might dine.

They each took a bumper,
   And drank to the pair,—
Cock Robin the bridegroom,
   And Jenny the fair.

I had a little husband,
　　No bigger than my thumb;
I put him in a pint-pot
　　And there I bade him drum.

I bought a little horse
　　That galloped up and down;
I bridled him, and saddled him
　　And sent him out of town.

I gave him some garters
　　To garter up his hose,
And a little silk handkerchief
　　To wipe his pretty nose.

Bobby Shafto's gone to sea,
　　Silver buckles at his knee;
He'll come back and marry me,
　　Pretty Bobby Shafto!

Bobby Shafto's fat and fair,
　　Combing down his yellow hair;
He's my love for evermore.
　　Pretty Bobby Shafto!

There was an old woman who lived in a shoe,
She had so many children she didn't know what to do;
She gave them some broth without any bread;
She whipped them all soundly and put them to bed.

Can you make me a cambric shirt,
    Parsley, sage, rosemary, and thyme,
Without any seam or needlework?
    And you shall be a true lover of mine.

    Can you wash it in yonder well,
        Parsley, sage, rosemary, and thyme,
    Where never sprung water, nor rain ever fell?
        And you shall be a true lover of mine.

        Can you dry it on yonder thorn,
           Parsley, sage, rosemary, and thyme,
        Which never bore blossom since Adam was born?
           And you shall be a true lover of mine.

              Now you've asked me questions three,
                Parsley, sage, rosemary, and thyme,
              I hope you'll answer as many for me,
                And you shall be a true lover of mine.

            Can you find me an acre of land,
              Parsley, sage, rosemary, and thyme,
            Between the salt water and the sea sand?
              And you shall be a true lover of mine.

              Can you plough it with a ram's horn,
                Parsley, sage, rosemary, and thyme,
              And sow it all over with one pepper-corn?
                And you shall be a true lover of mine.

Can you reap it with a sickle of leather,
  Parsley, sage, rosemary, and thyme,
And bind it up with a peacock's feather?
  And you shall be a true lover of mine.

When you have done and finished your work,
  Parsley, sage, rosemary, and thyme,
Then come to me for your cambric shirt,
  And you shall be a true lover of mine.

When a twister a-twisting, will twist him a twist,
For the twisting his twist, he three times doth intwist;
But if one of the twines of the twist do untwist,
The twine that untwisteth, untwisteth the twist.

Untwirling the twine that untwisteth between,
He twists, with the twister, the two in a twine;
Then twice having twisted the twines of the twine,
He twisteth the twine he had twined in twain.

The twain that, in twining, before in the twine,
As twines were intwisted, he now doth untwine;
'Twixt the twain intertwisting a twine more between,
He, twirling his twister, makes a twist of the twine.

37

There once were two cats of Kilkenny,
Each thought there was one cat too many;
So they fought and they fit,
And they scratched and they bit,
Till, excepting their nails
And the tips of their tails
Instead of two cats, there weren't any.

Mary had a little lamb,
  Its fleece was white as snow;
And everywhere that Mary went
  The lamb was sure to go.

It followed her to school one day,
  That was against the rule;
It made the children laugh and play
  To see a lamb at school.

And so the teacher turned it out,
  But still it lingered near;
And waited patiently about
  Till Mary did appear.

"Why does the lamb love Mary so?"
  The eager children cry.
"Why, Mary loves the lamb, you know,"
  The teacher did reply.

Young lambs to sell! Young lambs to sell!
I never would cry young lambs to sell,
If I'd as much money as I could tell
I never would cry young lambs to sell.

Hey diddle, dinketty, poppety, pet,
The merchants of London they wear scarlet,
Silk in the collar, gold in the hem,
So merrily march the merchantmen.

See-saw, Margery Daw,
Jacky shall have a new master;
Jacky must have but a penny a day,
Because he can't work any faster.

Oh, what have you got for dinner, Mrs. Bond?
There's beef in the larder, and ducks in the pond;
Dilly, dilly, dilly, dilly, come to be killed,
For you must be stuffed and my customers filled!

Send us the beef first, good Mrs. Bond,
And get us some ducks dressed out of the pond,
Cry, Dilly, dilly, dilly, dilly, come to be killed,
For you must be stuffed and my customers filled!

John Ostler, go fetch me a duckling or two,
Ma'am, says John Ostler, I'll try what I can do,
Cry, Dilly, dilly, dilly, dilly, come to be killed,
For you must be stuffed and my customers filled!

I have been to the ducks that swim in the pond,
But I found they won't come to be killed, Mrs. Bond;
I cried, Dilly, dilly, dilly, dilly, come to be killed,
For you must be stuffed and my customers filled!

Mrs. Bond she flew down to the pond in a rage,
With plenty of onions and plenty of sage;
She cried, Dilly, dilly, dilly, dilly, come to be killed,
For you must be stuffed and my customers filled!

She cried, Little wag-tails, come and be killed,
For you must be stuffed and my customers filled!
Dilly, dilly, dilly, dilly, come to be killed,
For you must be stuffed and my customers filled!

Hannah Bantry, in the pantry,
Gnawing at a mutton bone;
How she gnawed it,
How she clawed it,
When she found herself alone.

Once I saw a little bird
  Come hop, hop, hop,
And I cried, Little bird,
  Will you stop, stop, stop?

I was going to the window
  To say, How do you do?
But he shook his little tail
  And away he flew.

Dame Trot and her cat
Led a peaceable life,
When they were not troubled
With other folks' strife.

When Dame had her dinner,
Pussy would wait,
And was sure to receive
A nice piece from her plate.

A was an archer, who shot at a frog,
B was a butcher, and had a great dog.
C was a captain, all covered with lace,
D was a drunkard, and had a red face.
E was an esquire, with pride on his brow,
F was a farmer, and followed the plough.
G was a gamester, who had but ill-luck,
H was a hunter, and hunted a buck.
I was an innkeeper, who loved to carouse,
J was a joiner, and built up a house.
K was King William, once governed this land,
L was a lady, who had a white hand.
M was a miser, and hoarded up gold,
N was a nobleman, gallant and bold.
O was an oyster girl, and went about town,
P was a parson, and wore a black gown.
Q was a queen, who wore a silk slip,
R was a robber, and wanted a whip.
S was a sailor, and spent all he got,
T was a tinker, and mended a pot.
U was a usurer, a miserable elf,
V was a vintner, who drank all himself.
W was a watchman, and guarded the door,
X was expensive, and so became poor.
Y was a youth, that did not love school,
Z was a zany, a poor harmless fool.

Oh dear! what can the matter be?
Dear, dear! what can the matter be?
Oh dear! what can the matter be?
Johnny's so long at the fair.

He promised he'd buy me a fairing should please me,
And then for a kiss, oh! he vowed he would tease me,
He promised he'd bring me a bunch of blue ribbons
To tie up my bonny brown hair.

Oh dear! what can the matter be?
Dear, dear! what can the matter be?
Oh dear! what can the matter be?
Johnny's so long at the fair.

He promised he'd bring me a basket of posies,
A garland of lilies, a garland of roses,
A little straw hat, to set off the blue ribbons
That tie up my bonny brown hair.

Tom, he was a piper's son,
He learned to play when he was young,
And all the tune that he could play
Was, "Over the hills and far away,"
Over the hills and a great way off,
And the wind will blow my top-knot off.

Tom with his pipe made such a noise,
That he pleased both the girls and boys,
And they all stopped to hear him play,
"Over the hills and far away."

Tom with his pipe did play with such skill
That those who heard him could never keep still;
As soon as he played they began for to dance,
Even pigs on their hind legs would after him prance.

As Dolly was milking her cow one day,
Tom took his pipe and began for to play;
So Doll and the cow danced, "The Cheshire Round,"
Till the pail was broken and the milk ran on the ground.

He met old Dame Trot with a basket of eggs,
He used his pipe and she used her legs;
She danced about till the eggs were all broke,
She began for to fret, but he laughed at the joke.

Tom saw a cross fellow was beating an ass,
Heavy laden with pots, pans, dishes, and glass;
He took out his pipe and he played them a tune,
And the poor donkey's load was lightened full soon.

I've seen you where you never were,
And where you ne'er will be,
And yet you in that very same place,
May still be seen by me.

   ] *Reflection in a mirror*

If you sneeze on Monday, you sneeze for danger;
Sneeze on a Tuesday, kiss a stranger;
Sneeze on a Wednesday, sneeze for a letter;
Sneeze on a Thursday, something better;
Sneeze on a Friday, sneeze for sorrow;
Sneeze on a Saturday, see your sweetheart to-morrow.

Little lad, little lad, where wast thou born?
Far off in Lancashire, under a thorn,
Where they sup buttermilk from a ram's horn,
And a pumpkin scooped, with a yellow rim,
Is the bonny bowl they breakfast in.

Margery Mutton-pie and Johnny Bo-peep,
They met together in Gracechurch Street;
In and out, in and out, over the way,
"Oh," said Johnny, "it's chop-nose day."

Tom, Tom, the piper's son,
Stole a pig and away did run!
The pig was eat, and Tom was beat,
Till he ran crying down the street.

The fair maid who, the first of May,
Goes to the fields at break of day,
And washes in dew from the hawthorn tree,
Will ever after handsome be.

There was an old woman tossed up in a basket
    Nineteen times as high as the moon;
Where she was going I couldn't but ask it,
    For in her hand she carried a broom.

"Old woman, old woman, old woman," quoth I,
    "O whither, O whither, O whither, so high?"
"To brush the cobwebs off the sky!"
    "Shall I go with thee?" "Ay, by-and-by."

As I was going to Derby,
    Upon a market day,
I met the finest ram, sir,
    That ever was fed on hay.

This ram was fat behind, sir,
    This ram was fat before,
This ram was ten yards high, sir,
    Indeed he was no more.

The wool upon his back, sir,
    Reached up unto the sky,
The eagles build their nests there,
    For I heard the young ones cry.

The space between the horns, sir,
    Was as far as man could reach,
And there they built a pulpit,
    But no-one in it preached.

This ram had four legs to walk upon,
    This ram had four legs to stand,
And every leg he had, sir,
    Stood on an acre of land.

Indeed, sir, it's the truth, sir,
    For I never was taught to lie,
And if you go to Derby, sir,
    You may eat a bit of the pie.

Now the man that fed the ram, sir,
    He fed him twice a day,
And each time that he fed him, sir,
    He ate a rick of hay.

The man that killed this ram, sir,
    Was up to his knees in blood,
And the boy that held the pail, sir,
    Was carried away in the flood.

Here's a health to the barley mow;
Here's a health to the man
Who very well can
Both harrow, and plough, and sow.
When it is well sown,
See it is well mown,
Both raked and gravelled clean,
And a barn to lay it in;
Here's a health to the man
Who very well can
Both thresh and fan it clean.

Elsie Marley is grown so fine,
She won't get up to feed the swine,
But lies in bed till eight or nine.
Lazy Elsie Marley.

Little Betty Pringle she had a pig,
It was not very little and not very big;
When he was alive he lived in clover,
But now he's dead and that's all over.
Johnny Pringle he sat down and cried,
Betty Pringle she lay down and died;
So there was an end of one, two, three,
    Johnny Pringle he,
    Betty Pringle she,
    And Piggy Wiggy.

49

Dame, get up and bake your pies,
  Bake your pies, bake your pies;
Dame, get up and bake your pies,
  On Christmas day in the morning.

    Dame, what makes your maidens lie,
      Maidens lie, maidens lie;
    Dame, what makes your maidens lie,
      On Christmas day in the morning?

      Dame, what makes your ducks to die,
        Ducks to die, ducks to die;
      Dame, what makes your ducks to die,
        On Christmas day in the morning?

Their wings are cut and they cannot fly,
  Cannot fly, cannot fly;
Their wings are cut and they cannot fly,
  On Christmas day in the morning.

        Hark, hark,
        The dogs do bark,
        The beggars are coming to town;
        Some in rags,
        And some in tags,
        And one in a velvet gown.

Barber, barber, shave a pig,
How many hairs will make a wig?
"Four and twenty, that's enough."
Give the poor barber a pinch of snuff.

As I went through the garden gap,
Who should I meet but Dick Red-cap!
A stick in his hand, a stone in his throat,
If you'll tell me this riddle, I'll give you a groat.

]*A cherry*

If all the world were apple pie,
And all the seas were ink,
And all the trees were bread and cheese
What should we have for drink?

Here we go round the mulberry bush,
The mulberry bush, the mulberry bush,
Here we go round the mulberry bush,
On a cold and frosty morning.

This is the way we wash our hands,
Wash our hands, wash our hands,
This is the way we wash our hands,
On a cold and frosty morning.

This is the way we wash our clothes,
Wash our clothes, wash our clothes,
This is the way we wash our clothes,
On a cold and frosty morning.

This is the way we go to school,
Go to school, go to school,
This is the way we go to school,
On a cold and frosty morning.

This is the way we come out of school,
Come out of school, come out of school,
This is the way we come out of school,
On a cold and frosty morning.

Pussy sits beside the fire.
How can she be fair?
In walks a little doggy,—
Pussy, are you there?

I had a little dog and they called him Buff,
I sent him to a shop to buy me snuff,
But he lost the bag and spilt the stuff;
I sent him no more but gave him a cuff,
For coming from the mart without any snuff.

As I walked by myself
   And talked to myself,
   Myself said unto me:
   Look to thyself,
   Take care of thyself,
For nobody cares for thee.

   I answered myself
      And said to myself
   In the self-same repartee:
      Look to thyself
      Or not look to thyself,
   The self-same thing will be.

Four stiff-standers,
Four dilly-danders,
Two lookers, two crookers,
And a long wiggle-waggle.

                              ]*A cow*

Old Abram Brown is dead and gone,
You'll never see him more;
He used to wear a long brown coat
That buttoned down before.

Little Betty Blue
Lost her holiday shoe,
What can little Betty do?
Give her another
To match the other,
And then she may walk out in two.

As Tommy Snooks and Bessy Brooks
Were walking out one Sunday,
Says Tommy Snooks to Bessy Brooks,
Tomorrow will be Monday.

Little Nancy Etticoat,
With a white petticoat,
And a red nose;
She has no feet or hands,
The longer she stands
The shorter she grows.

55

A farmer went trotting upon his grey mare,
   Bumpety, bumpety, bump!
With his daughter behind him so rosy and fair,
   Lumpety, lumpety, lump!

A raven cried, Croak! and they all tumbled down,
   Bumpety, bumpety, bump!
The mare broke her knees and the farmer his crown,
   Lumpety, lumpety, lump!

The mischievous raven flew laughing away,
    Bumpety, bumpety, bump!
And vowed he would serve them the same the next day.
    Lumpety, lumpety, lump!

If all the seas were one sea,
What a *great* sea that would be!
If all the trees were one tree,
What a *great* tree that would be!
And if all the axes were one axe,
What a *great* axe that would be!
And if all the men were one man,
What a *great* man that would be!
And if the *great* man took the *great* axe,
And cut down the *great* tree,
And let it fall into the *great* sea,
What a splish-splash that would be!

Gregory Griggs, Gregory Griggs,
Had twenty-seven different wigs.
He wore them up, he wore them down,
To please the people of the town;
He wore them east, he wore them west,
But he never could tell which he loved the best.

Bounce, buckram, velvet's dear,
Christmas comes but once a year;
And when it comes, it brings good cheer,
But when it's gone it's never near.

Dickery, dickery, dare,
The pig flew up in the air;
The man in brown soon brought him down,
Dickery, dickery, dare.

Doctor Foster went to Gloucester
In a shower of rain;
He stepped in a puddle,
Right up to his middle,
And never went there again.

Fiddle de dee, fiddle de dee,
The fly has married the humble-bee.
They went to the church, and married was she.
The fly has married the humble-bee.

Fa, Fe, Fi, Fo, Fum!
I smell the blood of an Englishman:
Be he alive, or be he dead,
I'll grind his bones to make me bread.

Please to remember
The Fifth of November,
Gunpowder treason and plot!
For I see no reason
Why gunpowder treason
Should ever be forgot.

My Lady Wind, my Lady Wind,
Went round about the house, to find
A chink to get her foot in;
She tried the keyhole in the door,
She tried the crevice in the floor,
And drove the chimney soot in.

And then one night when it was dark,
She blew up such a tiny spark,
That all the house was pothered;
From it she raised up such a flame,
As flamed away to Belting Lane,
And White Cross folks were smothered.

And thus when once, my little dears,
A whisper reaches itching ears,—
The same will come, you'll find,—
Take my advice, restrain your tongue,
Remember what old nurse has sung
Of busy Lady Wind.

One, two, three, four, and five,
I caught a hare alive;
Six, seven, eight, nine, and ten,
I let him go again.

Every lady in this land
Has twenty nails upon each hand
Five and twenty hands and feet,
All this is true without deceit.

]*Mind the stops!*

There was an old woman
Lived under a hill,
And if she's not gone
She lives there still.

61

If I had a donkey that wouldn't go,
Would I beat him? Oh no, no.
I'd put him in the barn and give him some corn,
The best little donkey that ever was born.

Molly, my sister, and I fell out,
And what do you think it was all about?
She loved coffee and I loved tea,
And that was the reason we couldn't agree.

I had a little Hen, the prettiest ever seen,
She washed me the dishes, and kept the house clean.
She went to the mill to fetch me some flour;
She brought it home in less than an hour;
She baked me my bread, she brewed me my ale,
She sat by the fire and told many a fine tale.

I love sixpence, jolly little sixpence,
  I love sixpence better than my life;
I spent a penny of it, I lent a penny of it,
  And I took fourpence home to my wife.

    Oh, my little fourpence, jolly little fourpence,
      I love fourpence better than my life;
    I spent a penny of it, I lent a penny of it,
      And I took twopence home to my wife.

        Oh, my little twopence, jolly little twopence,
          I love twopence better than my life;
        I spent a penny of it, I lent a penny of it,
          And I took nothing home to my wife.

Oh, my little nothing, jolly little nothing,
  What will nothing buy for my wife?
I have nothing, I spend nothing,
  I love nothing better than my wife.

        Hinx, minx, the old witch winks,
        The fat begins to fry,
        Nobody at home but jumping Joan,
        Father, mother and I.
        Stick, stock, stone dead,
        Blind man can't see,
        Every knave will have a slave,
        You or I must be he.

As round as an apple,
As deep as a cup,
And all the king's horses
Cannot pull it up.
                              ]A well   63

A fox jumped up one winter's night,
And begged the moon to give him light,
For he'd many miles to trot that night
Before he reached his den O!
    Den O!   Den O!
For he'd many miles to trot that night
Before he reached his den O!

The first place he came to was a farmer's yard,
Where the ducks and the geese declared it hard
That their nerves should be shaken and their rest so marred
By a visit from Mr. Fox O!
    Fox O!   Fox O!
That their nerves should be shaken and their rest so marred
By a visit from Mr. Fox O!

He took the grey goose by the neck,
And swung him right across his back;
The grey goose cried out, Quack, quack, quack,
With his legs hanging dangling down O!
    Down O!   Down O!
The grey goose cried out, Quack, quack, quack,
With his legs hanging dangling down O!

Old Mother Slipper Slopper jumped out of bed,
And out of the window she popped her head:
Oh! John, John, John, the grey goose is gone,
And the fox is off to his den O!
    Den O!   Den O!
Oh! John, John, John, the grey goose is gone,
And the fox is off to his den O!

John ran up to the top of the hill,
And blew his whistle loud and shrill;
Said the fox, That is very pretty music; still—
I'd rather be in my den O!
   Den O!   Den O!
Said the fox, That is very pretty music; still—
I'd rather be in my den O!

The fox went back to his hungry den,
And his dear little foxes, eight, nine, ten;
Quoth they, Good daddy, you must go there again,
If you bring such good cheer from the farm O!
   Farm O!   Farm O!
Quoth they, Good daddy, you must go there again,
If you bring such good cheer from the farm O!

The fox and his wife, without any strife,
Said they never ate a better goose in all their life;
They did very well without fork or knife,
And the little ones picked the bones O!
   Bones O!   Bones O!
They did very well without fork or knife,
And the little ones picked the bones O!

Whistle, daughter, whistle,
  And you shall have a sheep.
Mother, I cannot whistle,
  Neither can I sleep.

Whistle, daughter, whistle,
  And you shall have a cow.
Mother, I cannot whistle,
  Neither know I how.

Whistle, daughter, whistle,
  And you shall have a man.
Mother, I cannot whistle,
  But I'll do the best I can.

I would if I could,
If I couldn't, how could I?
I couldn't without I could, could I?
Could you, without you could, could ye?
Could ye, could-ye?
Could you, without you could, could ye?

Ladybird, ladybird
  Fly away home,
Your house is on fire
  And your children all gone;
All except one
  And that's little Ann
And she has crept under
  The warming pan.

Old chairs to mend! Old chairs to mend!
I never would cry old chairs to mend,
If I'd as much money as I could spend,
I never would cry old chairs to mend.

    Old clothes to sell! Old clothes to sell!
    I never would cry old clothes to sell,
    If I'd as much money as I could tell,
    I never would cry old clothes to sell.

        He that would thrive,
        Must rise at five;
        He that has thriven,
        May lie till seven;
        And he that by the plough would thrive,
        Himself must either hold or drive.

It costs little Gossip her income for shoes,
To travel about and carry the news.

Thomas a Tattamus took two tees,
To tie two tups to two tall trees,
To frighten the terrible Thomas a Tattamus!
Tell me how many T's there are in that.

Tweedledum and Tweedledee
   Resolved to have a battle,
For Tweedledum said Tweedledee
   Had spoiled his nice new rattle.

Just then flew by a monstrous crow,
   As big as a tar-barrel,
Which frightened both the heroes so,
   They quite forgot their quarrel.

Over the water and over the lea,
　And over the water to Charley.
Charley loves good ale and wine,
　And Charley loves good brandy,
And Charley loves a pretty girl
　As sweet as sugar candy.

　　Over the water and over the lea,
　　　And over the water to Charley.
　　I'll have none of your nasty beef,
　　　Nor I'll have none of your barley;
　　But I'll have some of your very best flour
　　　To make a white cake for my Charley.

　　Peter Piper picked a peck of pickled pepper;
　　A peck of pickled pepper Peter Piper picked;
　　If Peter Piper picked a peck of pickled pepper,
　　Where's the peck of pickled pepper Peter Piper picked?

Come when you're called,
　Do as you're bid,
Shut the door after you,
　Never be chid.

　　　Four and twenty tailors
　　　　Went to kill a snail,
　　　The best man among them
　　　　Durst not touch her tail;
　　　She put out her horns
　　　　Like a little Kyloe cow.
　　　Run, tailors, run
　　　　Or she'll kill you all e'en now.　69

Gay go up and gay go down,
To ring the bells of London Town.

Bull's eyes and targets,
Say the bells of St. Margaret's.

Brickbats and tiles,
Say the bells of St. Giles'.

Halfpence and farthings,
Say the bells of St. Martin's.

Oranges and lemons,
Say the bells of St. Clement's.

Pancakes and fritters,
Say the bells of St. Peter's.

Two sticks and an apple,
Say the bells at Whitechapel.

Old Father Baldpate,
Say the slow bells at Aldgate.

Pokers and tongs,
Say the bells of St. John's.

Kettles and pans,
Say the bells of St. Anne's.

You owe me ten shillings,
Say the bells of St. Helen's.

When will you pay me?
Say the bells at Old Bailey.

When I grow rich,
Say the bells at Shoreditch.

Pray when will that be?
Say the bells of Stepney.

I am sure I don't know,
Says the great bell at Bow.

Here comes a candle to light you to bed,
And here comes a chopper to chop off your head.

There was a little girl, and she had a little curl
  Right in the middle of her forehead;
When she was good, she was very, very good,
  But when she was bad, she was horrid.

God bless the master of this house,
Likewise the mistress too,
And all the little children
That round the table go;

And all your kin and kinsmen,
That dwell both far and near;
I wish you a Merry Christmas,
And a Happy New Year.

,The first day of Christmas,
My true love sent to me
A partridge in a pear tree.

The second day of Christmas,
My true love sent to me
Two turtle doves, and
A partridge in a pear tree.

The third day of Christmas,
My true love sent to me
Three French hens,
Two turtle doves, and
A partridge in a pear tree.

The fourth day of Christmas,
My true love sent to me
Four colly birds,
Three French hens,
Two turtle doves, and
A partridge in a pear tree.

The fifth day of Christmas,
My true love sent to me
Five gold rings,
Four colly birds,
Three French hens,
Two turtle doves, and
A partridge in a pear tree.

The sixth day of Christmas,
My true love sent to me
Six geese a-laying,
Five gold rings,
Four colly birds,
Three French hens,
Two turtle doves, and
A partridge in a pear tree.

The seventh day of Christmas,
My true love sent to me
Seven swans a-swimming,
Six geese a-laying,
Five gold rings,
Four colly birds,
Three French hens,
Two turtle doves, and
A partridge in a pear tree.

The eighth day of Christmas,
My true love sent to me
Eight maids a-milking,
Seven swans a-swimming,
Six geese a-laying,
Five gold rings,
Four colly birds,
Three French hens,
Two turtle doves, and
A partridge in a pear tree.

The ninth day of Christmas,
My true love sent to me
Nine drummers drumming,
Eight maids a-milking,
Seven swans a-swimming,
Six geese a-laying,
Five gold rings,
Four colly birds,
Three French hens,
Two turtle doves, and
A partridge in a pear tree.   73

The tenth day of Christmas,
My true love sent to me
Ten pipers piping,
Nine drummers drumming,
Eight maids a-milking,
Seven swans a-swimming,
Six geese a-laying,
Five gold rings,
Four colly birds,
Three French hens,
Two turtle doves, and
A partridge in a pear tree.

The eleventh day of Christmas,
My true love sent to me
Eleven ladies dancing,
Ten pipers piping,
Nine drummers drumming,
Eight maids a-milking,
Seven swans a-swimming,
Six geese a-laying,
Five gold rings,
Four colly birds,
Three French hens,
Two turtle doves, and
A partridge in a pear tree.

The twelfth day of Christmas,
My true love sent to me
Twelve lords a-leaping,
Eleven ladies dancing,
Ten pipers piping,
Nine drummers drumming,
Eight maids a-milking,
Seven swans a-swimming,
Six geese a-laying,
Five gold rings,
Four colly birds,
Three French hens,
Two turtle doves, and
A partridge in a pear tree.

Christmas comes but once a year,
And when it comes it brings good cheer.

Some little mice sat in a barn to spin;
Pussy came by, and popped her head in:
"What are you doing my little men?"
"Weaving coats for gentlemen."
"Shall I come in, and cut your threads off?"
"Oh, no! kind sir, you will snap our heads off!"

Says Puss: "You look so wondrous wise,
I like your whiskers and bright black eyes;
Your house is the nicest house I see,
I think there is room for you and me."
The mice were so pleased, that they opened the door,
And pussy soon laid them all dead on the floor.

Little King Pippin he built a fine hall,
Pie-crust and pastry-crust that was the wall;
The windows were made of black pudding and white,
And slated with pancakes, you ne'er saw the like.

My dear, do you know,
How a long time ago,
Two poor little children,
Whose names I don't know,
Were stolen away
On a fine summer's day,
And left in a wood,
As I've heard people say.
Poor babes in the wood! poor babes in the wood!
Oh! don't you remember the babes in the wood?

And when it was night,
So sad was their plight,
The sun it went down,
And the moon gave no light!
They sobbed and they sighed,
And they bitterly cried,
And the poor little things,
They lay down and died.
Poor babes in the wood! poor babes in the wood!
Oh, don't you remember the babes in the wood?

And when they were dead,
The robins so red
Brought strawberry leaves,
And over them spread;
And all the day long,
The branches among,
They mournfully whistled,
And this was their song:
Poor babes in the wood! poor babes in the wood!
Oh! don't you remember the babes in the wood?

Mistress Mary, quite contrary,
    How does your garden grow?
With silver bells and cockle shells,
    And pretty maids all in a row.

The cat sat asleep by the side of the fire,
    The mistress snored loud as a pig;
Jack took up his fiddle by Jenny's desire,
    And struck up a bit of a jig.

Cock-a-doodle-doo!
My dame has lost her shoe,
My master's lost his fiddlestick,
And knows not what to do.

Cock-a-doodle-doo!
What is my dame to do?
Till master finds his fiddlestick,
She'll dance without her shoe.

Come hither, little puppy dog;
    I'll give you a new collar
If you will learn to read your book,
    And be a clever scholar.

"No, no!" replied the puppy dog,
    "I've other fish to fry,
For I must learn to guard your house,
    And bark when thieves come nigh."

With a tingle, tangle, tit-mouse!
    Robin knows great A
And B and C and D and E,
        F, G, H, I, J, K.

Come hither, pretty cockatoo;
    Come and learn your letters,
And you shall have a knife and fork
    To eat with, like your betters.

"No, no!" the cockatoo replied,
    "My beak will do as well;
I'd rather eat my victuals thus
    Than go and learn to spell."

With a tingle, tangle, tit-mouse!
    Robin knows great A
And B and C and D and E,
        F, G, H, I, J, K.

Come hither, little pussy cat;
    If you'll your grammar study,
I'll give you silver clogs to wear
    Whene'er the gutter's muddy.

"No! whilst I grammar learn," says Puss,
    "Your house will, in a trice,
Be overrun from top to bottom
    With flocks of rats and mice."

With a tingle, tangle, tit-mouse!
  Robin knows great A
And B and C and D and E,
      F, G, H, I, J, K.

    Come hither, then, good little boy,
      And learn your alphabet,
    And then a pair of boots and spurs
      Like Papa's you shall get.

     "Oh, yes! I'll learn my alphabet;
       And when I well can read,
     Perhaps Papa will give me, too,
       A pretty long-tailed steed."

With a tingle, tangle, tit-mouse!
  Robin knows great A
And B and C and D and E,
      F, G, H, I, J, K.

      My little old man and I fell out,
      How shall we bring this matter about?
      Bring it about as well as you can,
      And get you gone, you little old man!

Sing, sing, what shall I sing:
The cat's run away with the pudding string!
Do, do, what shall I do?
The cat has bitten it quite in two!

The cock's on the wood pile a-blowing his horn,
The bull's in the barn a-threshing of corn,
The maids in the meadows are making of hay,
The ducks in the river are swimming away.

Oh! the grand old Duke of York,
He had ten thousand men;
He marched them up to the top of a hill,
And he marched them down again!

And when they were up, they were up,
And when they were down, they were down,
And when they were only half way up,
They were neither up nor down.

I had a little nut tree,
　　Nothing would it bear
But a silver nutmeg
　　And a golden pear;

　　The King of Spain's daughter
　　　　Came to visit me,
　　And all for the sake
　　　　Of my little nut tree.

　　　　I skipped over water,
　　　　　I danced over sea,
　　　　And all the birds in the air
　　　　　Couldn't catch me.

There was a jolly miller
　　Lived on the river Dee:
He worked and sung from morn till night,
　　No lark so blithe as he;
And this the burden of his song
　　For ever used to be:—
I jump mejerrime jee!
　　I care for nobody—no! not I,
Since nobody cares for me.

Bessy Bell and Mary Gray,
They were two bonny lasses;
They built their house upon the lea,
And covered it with rushes.

Bessy kept the garden gate,
And Mary kept the pantry;
Bessy always had to wait,
While Mary lived in plenty.

Hush-a-bye, baby, on the tree top,
When the wind blows the cradle will rock;
When the bough breaks the cradle will fall,
Down will come baby, cradle, and all.

Bye, baby bunting,
Daddy's gone a-hunting,
To get a little rabbit's skin,
To wrap a baby bunting in.

Hush thee, my babby,
Lie still with thy daddy,
Thy mammy has gone to the mill,
To grind thee some wheat
To make thee some meat,
Oh, my dear babby, lie still.

Hush-a-bye, baby,
Daddy is near,
Mammy's a lady,
And that's very clear.

84

Dance, little baby, dance up high:
Never mind, baby, mother is by;
Crow and caper, caper and crow,
There, little baby, there you go;

Up to the ceiling, down to the ground,
Backwards and forwards, round and round:
Dance, little baby, and mother shall sing,
With the merry gay choral, ding, ding-a-ding, ding.

One, two,
Buckle my shoe;
Three, four,
Knock at the door;
Five, six,
Pick up sticks;
Seven, eight,
Lay them straight;
Nine, ten,
A big fat hen;
Eleven, twelve,
Dig and delve;
Thirteen, fourteen,
Maids a-courting;
Fifteen, sixteen,
Maids in the kitchen;
Seventeen, eighteen,
Maids in waiting;
Nineteen, twenty,
My plate's empty.

Brow, brow, brinkie,
Eye, eye, winkie,
Mouth, mouth, merry,
Cheek, cheek, cherry,
Chin-chopper, chin-chopper.

Ring the bell!
Knock at the door!
Lift up the latch!
And walk in!

] *Baby's face*

Cry, baby, cry,
Put your finger in your eye,
And tell your mother it wasn't I.

85

To market, to market,
To buy a plum bun:
Home again, home again,
Market is done.

To market, to market, to buy a fat pig,
Home again, home again, jiggety-jig;

To market, to market, to buy a fat hog,
Home again, home again, jiggety-jog.

Pat-a-cake, pat-a-cake, baker's man,
Bake me a cake as fast as you can;
Pat it and prick it, and mark it with B,
Put it in the oven for baby and me.

Great A, little A,
This is pancake day;
Toss the ball high,
Throw the ball low,
Those that come after
May sing Heigh-ho!

Ride a cock-horse to Banbury Cross,
To see a fine lady upon a white horse;
Rings on her fingers and bells on her toes,
And she shall have music wherever she goes.

Great A, little a,
　　Bouncing B,
The cat's in the cupboard
　　And can't see me.

Pease porridge hot,
Pease porridge cold,
Pease porridge in the pot
Nine days old.

Some like it hot,
Some like it cold,
Some like it in the pot
Nine days old.

]A game for hands

This little pig went to market,
This little pig stayed at home,
This little pig had roast beef,
This little pig had none,
And this little pig cried, Wee-wee-wee-wee-wee,
　　I can't find my way home.

]A rhyme for five Toes

Here's Sulky Sue,
What shall we do?
Turn her face to the wall
Till she comes to.

Shoe a little horse,
Shoe a little mare,
But let the little coltie go bare, bare, bare.

I see the moon,
    And the moon sees me;
God bless the moon,
    And God bless me.

Hey, my kitten, my kitten,
    And hey my kitten, my deary!
Such a sweet pet as this
    Was neither far nor neary.

Here we go up, up, up,
    Here we go down, down, downy;
Here we go backwards and forwards,
    And here we go round, round, roundy.

Here is the church, and here is the steeple;
Open the door and here are the people.
Here is the parson going upstairs,
And here he is a-saying his prayers.
                    ]*Finger game*   89

Cuckoo, cherry tree,
Catch a bird, and give it to me;
Let the tree be high or low,
Let it hail, rain, or snow.

Dance to your Daddy,
My little babby;
Dance to your Daddy,
  My little lamb.

You shall have a fishy
In a little dishy;
You shall have a fishy
  When the boat comes in.

Here sits the Lord Mayor,
                          ] forehead
Here sit his men,
                          ] eyes
Here sits the cockadoodle,
                          ] right cheek
Here sits the hen,
                          ] left cheek
Here sit the little chickens,
                          ] tip of the nose
Here they run in,
                          ] mouth
Chin chopper, chin chopper, chin chopper, chin.
                          ] chuck the chin

Rock-a-bye, baby,
  Thy cradle is green,
Father's a nobleman,
  Mother's a queen;
And Betty's a lady,
  And wears a gold ring;
And Johnny's a drummer,
  And drums for the king.

90

Dance, Thumbkin, dance,

] *keep the thumb moving*

Dance, ye merrymen, every one.

] *move all fingers*

For Thumbkin, he can dance alone,
Thumbkin, he can dance alone.

] *the thumb alone moving*

Dance, Foreman, dance,

] *first finger moving*

Dance, ye merrymen, every one.

] *all moving*

For Foreman, he can dance alone,
Foreman, he can dance alone.

] *first finger moving*

Dance, Longman, dance,

] *second finger moving*

Dance, ye merrymen, every one.

] *all moving*

For Longman, he can dance alone,
Longman, he can dance alone.

] *the second finger moving*

Dance, Ringman, dance,

] *third finger moving*

Dance, ye merrymen, every one.

] *all moving*

For Ringman he can dance alone,
Ringman, he can dance alone.

] *third finger moving*

Dance, Littleman, dance,

] *fourth finger moving*

Dance, ye merrymen, every one

] *all moving*

But Littleman cannot dance alone,
Littleman cannot dance alone.

] *the fourth finger erect*

Eye winker,
Tom Tinker,
Nose dropper,
Mouth eater,
Chin-chopper, chin-chopper.

] *Baby's face*

Brow bender,
Eye peeper,
Nose dreeper,
Mouth eater,
Chin chopper,
Knock at the door,
Ring the bell,
Lift up the latch,
Walk in . . .
Take a chair
Sit by there,
How d'you do this morning?

] *Baby's face*

91

There was an old man who lived in a wood,
  As you may plainly see;
He said he could do as much work in a day,
  As his wife could do in three.

  "With all my heart," the old woman said,
    "If that you will allow,
  To-morrow you'll stay at home in my stead,
    And I'll go drive the plough.

  "But you must milk the Tidy cow,
    For fear that she goes dry;
  And you must feed the little pigs,
    That are within the sty;

"And you must mind the speckled hen,
  For fear she lay astray;
And you must reel the spool of yarn
  That I spun yesterday."

  The old woman took a staff in her hand,
    And went to drive the plough;
  The old man took a pail in his hand,
    And went to milk the cow.

  But Tidy hinched, and Tidy flinched,
    And Tidy broke his nose;
  And Tidy gave him such a blow,
    That the blood ran down to his toes.

  "Hi, Tidy! ho, Tidy! hi!
    Tidy do stand still!
  If ever I milk you, Tidy, again,
    'Twill be sore against my will."

  He went to feed the little pigs,
    That were within the sty;
  He hit his head against the beam,
    And he made the blood to fly. 93

He went to mind the speckled hen,
    For fear she'd lay astray;
And he forgot the spool of yarn
    His wife spun yesterday.

So he swore by the sun, the moon, and the stars,
    And the green leaves on the tree,
If his wife didn't do a day's work in her life,
    She should ne'er be ruled by he.

What are little boys made of, made of?
What are little boys made of?
"Snips and snails, and puppy-dogs' tails;
And that's what little boys are made of, made of."

What are little girls made of, made of, made of?
What are little girls made of?
"Sugar and spice, and all that's nice;
And that's what little girls are made of, made of."

Pussy cat, pussy cat, where have you been?
I've been to London to look at the queen.
Pussy cat, pussy cat, what did you there?
I frightened a little mouse under her chair.

How many miles to Babylon?
Three score miles and ten.
Can I get there by candle-light?

Yes, and back again.
If your heels are nimble and light,
You may get there by candle-light.

A woman, a spaniel, and walnut tree,
The more you beat them the better they be.

I have a little sister, they call her Peep, Peep;
She wades the waters, deep, deep, deep;
She climbs the mountains high, high, high:
Poor little creature, she has but one eye!

]*A star*

There was a crooked man, and he walked a crooked mile.
He found a crooked sixpence against a crooked stile;
He bought a crooked cat, which caught a crooked mouse,
And they all lived together in a little crooked house.

Willy boy, Willy boy, where are you going?
    I will go with you, if that I may.
I'm going to the meadow to see them a-mowing,
    I am going to help them to make the hay.

Poor old Robinson Crusoe!
Poor old Robinson Crusoe!
They made him a coat of an old Nanny-goat,
I wonder how they could do so!
With a ring-a ting-a-tang, and a-ting-a-tang,
Poor old Robinson Crusoe!

There was a man and his name was Dob,
And he had a wife, and her name was Mob,
And he had a dog, and he called it Cob,
And she had a cat, called Chitterabob.
    "Cob," says Dob,
    "Chitterabob," says Mob,
    Cob was Dob's dog,
    Chitterabob Mob's cat.

To make your candles last for aye,
You wives and maids give ear O!
To put them out is the only way,
Says honest John Boldero.

Little Johnny Morgan,
   Gentleman of Wales,
Came riding on a nanny-goat,
   Selling of pigs' tails.

When I was a little boy I lived by myself,
And all the bread and cheese I got I laid upon a shelf;
The rats and the mice they made such a strife,
I had to go to London-town and buy me a wife.

The streets were so broad and the lanes were so narrow,
I was forced to bring my wife home in a wheelbarrow.
The wheelbarrow broke and my wife had a fall,
Farewell wheelbarrow, little wife and all.

In a cottage in Fife
Lived a man and his wife,
Who, believe me, were comical folk;
For, to people's surprise,
They both saw with their eyes,
And their tongues moved whenever they spoke!

When quite fast asleep,
I've been told that to keep
Their eyes open they could not contrive:
They walked on their feet,
And 'twas thought what they eat
Helped, with drinking, to keep them alive!

Little Tommy Tittlemouse
Lived in a little house;
He caught fishes
In other men's ditches.

March winds and April showers
Bring forth May flowers.

Jack and Jill went up the hill
    To fetch a pail of water;
Jack fell down and broke his crown,
    And Jill came tumbling after.

Up got Jack, and home did trot,
    As fast as he could caper,
To old Dame Dob, who patched his nob
    With vinegar and brown paper.

There was an old woman called Nothing-at-all,
Who rejoiced in a dwelling exceedingly small;
A man stretched his mouth to its utmost extent,
And down at one gulp house and old woman went.

I do not like thee, Doctor Fell,
The reason why I cannot tell;
But this I know, and know full well,
I do not like thee, Doctor Fell.

Here comes a poor woman from Baby-land,
With three small children in her hand:
One can brew, the other can bake,
The other can make a pretty round cake;
One can sit in the garden and spin,
Another can make a fine bed for the king.
Pray, ma'am, will you take one in?

The King of France went up the hill
With forty thousand men;
The King of France came down the hill,
And ne'er went up again.

Two legs sat upon three legs
With one leg in his lap;
In comes four legs
And runs away with one leg;
Up jumps two legs,
Catches up three legs,
Throws it after four legs,
And makes him bring back one leg.

Johnny Armstrong killed a calf,
Peter Henderson got half,
Willy Wilkinson got the head,
Ring the bell, the calf is dead.

Hickory, dickory, dock,
The mouse ran up the clock.
The clock struck one,
The mouse ran down,
Hickory, dickory, dock.

Jack be nimble,
Jack be quick,
Jack jump over
The candle stick.

I have four sisters beyond the sea,
    Perrie, Merrie, Dixie, Dominie;
And they each sent a present to me,
    Petrum, Partrum, Paradisi, Temporie,
    Perrie, Merrie, Dixie, Dominie.

The first sent a chicken, without e'er a bone,
    Perrie, Merrie, Dixie, Dominie;
The second a cherry, without e'er a stone,
    Petrum, Partrum, Paradisi, Temporie,
    Perrie, Merrie, Dixie, Dominie.

The third sent a book which no man could read,
    Perrie, Merrie, Dixie, Dominie;
The fourth sent a blanket without e'er a thread,
    Petrum, Partrum, Paradisi, Temporie,
    Perrie, Merrie, Dixie, Dominie.

How can there be a chicken without e'er a bone?
    Perrie, Merrie, Dixie, Dominie;
How can there be a cherry without e'er a stone?
    Petrum, Partrum, Paradisi, Temporie,
    Perrie, Merrie, Dixie, Dominie.

How can there be a book which no man can read?
    Perrie, Merrie, Dixie, Dominie;
How can there be a blanket without e'er a thread?
    Petrum, Partrum, Paradisi, Temporie,
    Perrie, Merrie, Dixie, Dominie.

When the chicken's in the egg-shell there is no bone,
    Perrie, Merrie, Dixie, Dominie;
When the cherry's in bud, there is no stone,
    Petrum, Partrum, Paradisi, Temporie,
    Perrie, Merrie, Dixie, Dominie.

When the book's in the press, no man it can read,
    Perrie, Merrie, Dixie, Dominie;
When the blanket's in the fleece there is no thread,
    Petrum, Partrum, Paradisi, Temporie,
    Perrie, Merrie, Dixie, Dominie.

Hickety, pickety, my black hen,
She lays eggs for gentlemen;
Gentlemen come every day
To see what my black hen doth lay.
Sometimes nine and sometimes ten,
Hickety, pickety, my black hen.

Tell-tale-tit!
Your tongue shall be slit,
And all the dogs in the town
Shall have a little bit.

Hot boiled beans and very good butter,
Ladies and gentlemen come to supper.

There was a man and he had nought,
    And robbers came to rob him;
He crept up to the chimney pot,
    And then they thought they had him.

But he got down on t'other side,
    And then they could not find him;
He ran fourteen miles in fifteen days,
    And never looked behind him.

Three little kittens they lost their mittens,
    And they began to cry,
"Oh, mother dear, we sadly fear
    That we have lost our mittens."
"What! lost your mittens, you naughty kittens!
    Then you shall have no pie."
    Mee-ow, mee-ow, mee-ow.
    No, you shall have no pie.

The three little kittens they found their mittens,
    And they began to cry,
"Oh, mother dear, see here, see here,
    For we have found our mittens."
"Put on your mittens, you silly kittens,
    And you shall have some pie."
    Purr-r, purr-r, purr-r,
    Oh, let us have some pie.

The three little kittens put on their mittens,
    And soon ate up the pie;
"Oh, mother dear, we greatly fear
    That we have soiled our mittens."
"What! soiled your mittens, you naughty kittens!"
    Then they began to sigh.
    Mee-ow, mee-ow, mee-ow.
    Then they began to sigh.

The three little kittens they washed their mittens,
    And hung them out to dry;
"Oh! mother dear, do you not hear
    That we have washed our mittens?"
"What! washed your mittens, then you're good kittens,
    But I smell a rat close by."
    Mee-ow, mee-ow, mee-ow.
    We smell a rat close by.

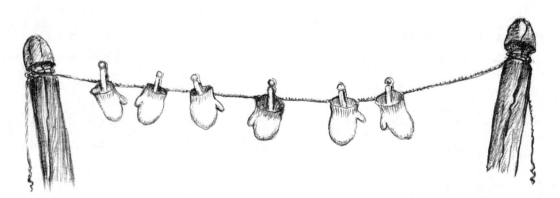

Where are you going to, my pretty maid?
I'm going a-milking, sir, she said,

Sir, she said, sir, she said,
I'm going a-milking, sir, she said.

May I go with you, my pretty maid?
You're kindly welcome, sir, she said.

Say, will you marry me, my pretty maid?
Yes, if you please, kind sir, she said.

What is your father, my pretty maid?
My father's a farmer, sir, she said.

What is your fortune, my pretty maid?
My face is my fortune, sir, she said.

One for anger,
Two for mirth,
Three for a wedding,
Four for a birth,
Five for rich,
Six for poor,
Seven for a witch,
I can tell you no more.

Then I can't marry you, my pretty maid.
Nobody asked you, sir, she said.

106

The lion and the unicorn
  Were fighting for the crown;
The lion beat the unicorn
  All round about the town.

If a man who turnips cries,
Cries not when his father dies,
It's a proof that he would rather
Have a turnip than a father.

Punch and Judy
  Fought for a pie;
Punch gave Judy
  A knock in the eye.

Says Punch to Judy
  Will you have any more?
Says Judy to Punch,
  My eye is sore.

Birds of a feather flock together,
  And so will pigs and swine;
Rats and mice will have their choice,
  And so will I have mine.

Old Mother Hubbard,
Went to the cupboard,
    To get her poor Dog a bone,
But when she got there,
The cupboard was bare,
    And so the poor Dog had none.

She went to the baker's
    To buy him some bread,
But when she came back
    The poor Dog was dead.

She went to the joiner's
    To buy him a coffin,
But when she came back
    The poor Dog was laughing.

She took a clean dish
    To get him some tripe,
But when she came back
    He was smoking a pipe.

She went to the fishmonger's
    To buy him some fish,
But when she came back
    He was licking the dish.

She went to the alehouse
    To get him some beer,
But when she came back
    The Dog sat in a chair.

She went to the tavern
    For white wine and red,
But when she came back
    The Dog stood on his head.

She went to the hatter's
To buy him a hat,
But when she came back
He was feeding the cat.

She went to the barber's
To buy him a wig;
But when she came back
He was dancing a jig.

She went to the fruiterer's
To buy him some fruit,
But when she came back
He was playing the flute.

She went to the tailor's
To buy him a coat,
But when she came back
He was riding a goat.

She went to the cobbler's
To buy him some shoes,
But when she came back
He was reading the news.

Deedle, deedle, dumpling, my son John,
Went to bed with his trousers on;
One shoe off, and one shoe on,
Deedle, deedle, dumpling, my son John.

If ifs and ands
Were pots and pans,
There would be no need for tinkers!

Hector Protector was dressed all in green;
Hector Protector was sent to the Queen.
The Queen did not like him,
No more did the King;
So Hector Protector was sent back again.

I saw a peacock with a fiery tail
I saw a blazing comet drop down hail
I saw a cloud with ivy circled round
I saw a sturdy oak creep on the ground
I saw a pismire swallow up a whale
I saw a raging sea brim full of ale
I saw a Venice glass sixteen foot deep
I saw a well full of men's tears that weep
I saw their eyes all in a flame of fire
I saw a house as big as the moon and higher
I saw the sun even in the midst of night
I saw the man that saw this wondrous sight.

Ring-a-ring o' roses,
A pocket full of posies,
   A-tishoo! A-tishoo!
We all fall down.

Multiplication is vexation,
Division is as bad;
The Rule of Three perplexes me,
And practice drives me mad.

Little Jack Jingle
He used to live single;
But when he got tired of this kind of life,
He left off being single and lived with his wife.
Now what do you think of little Jack Jingle?
Before he was married he used to live single.

As I was going to St. Ives,
I met a man with seven wives,
Each wife had seven sacks,
Each sack had seven cats,
Each cat had seven kits:
Kits, cats, sacks, and wives,
How many were there going to St. Ives?

As I was going along, long, long,
A-singing a comical song, song, song,
The lane that I went was so long, long, long,
And the song that I sung was as long, long, long,
And so I went singing along.

When the wind is in the East,
'Tis neither good for man nor beast;
When the wind is in the North,
The skilful fisher goes not forth;
When the wind is in the South,
It blows the bait in the fishes' mouth;
When the wind is in the West,
Then 'tis at the very best.

A cat came fiddling out of a barn,
With a pair of bagpipes under her arm;
She could sing nothing but "Fiddle cum fee,
The mouse has married the bumble bee."
Pipe Cat, Dance Mouse;
We'll have a wedding at our good house.

113

An apple a day
Sends the doctor away.

Apple in the morning,
Doctor's warning.

Roast apple at night,
Starves the doctor outright.

Three each day, seven days a week,
Ruddy apple, ruddy cheek.

Little miss, pretty miss,
Blessings light upon you!
If I had half a crown a day,
I'd spend it all upon you.

A swarm of bees in May
Is worth a load of hay;
A swarm of bees in June
Is worth a silver spoon;
A swarm of bees in July
Is not worth a fly.

Burn ash-wood green,
'Tis a fire for a queen;
Burn ash-wood sere,
'Twill make a man swear.

Three children sliding on the ice,
Upon a summer's day,
As it fell out, they all fell in,
The rest they ran away.

Now had these children been at home,
Or sliding on dry ground,
Ten thousand pounds to one penny
They had not all been drowned.

You parents all that children have,
And you that have got none,
If you would have them safe abroad,
Pray keep them safe at home.

See-Saw, Margery Daw,
The old hen flew over the malt-house;
She counted her chickens one by one,
Still she missed the little white one,
And this is it, this is it, this is it. 115

Of all the gay birds that e'er I did see,
The owl is the fairest by far to me:
For all the day long she sits in a tree,
And when the night comes away flies she.

A wise old owl lived in an oak;
The more he saw the less he spoke;
The less he spoke the more he heard.
Why can't we all be like that wise old bird?

Three blind mice, see how they run!
They all ran after the farmer's wife,
Who cut off their tails with a carving knife,
Did you ever see such a thing in your life,
    As three blind mice?

Robert Barnes, fellow fine,
Can you shoe this horse of mine?
Yes, good sir, that I can,
As well as any other man.
There's a nail, and there's a prod.
And now, good sir, your horse is shod.

When good King Arthur ruled this land,
  He was a goodly king;
He stole three pecks of barley-meal
  To make a bag-pudding.

A bag-pudding the king did make,
  And stuffed it well with plums;
And in it put great lumps of fat,
  As big as my two thumbs.

The king and queen did eat thereof,
  And noblemen beside;
And what they could not eat that night,
  The queen next morning fried.

We are all in the dumps,
  For diamonds are trumps;
The kittens are gone to St. Paul's!
  The babies are bit,
  The moon's in a fit,
And the houses are built without walls.

If wishes were horses,
  Then beggars would ride;
If turnips were watches,
  I'd wear one by my side.

See a pin and pick it up;
All the day you'll have good luck;
See a pin and let it lie,
Sure you'll want before you die.

Monday's child is fair of face,
Tuesday's child is full of grace,
Wednesday's child is full of woe,
Thursday's child has far to go,
Friday's child is loving and giving,
Saturday's child works hard for his living,
And the child that is born on the Sabbath day
Is bonny and blithe, and good and gay.

Simple Simon met a pieman
    Going to the fair;
Says Simple Simon to the pieman,
    "Let me taste your ware."

Says the pieman to Simple Simon,
    "Show me first your penny;"
Says Simple Simon to the pieman,
    "Indeed, I have not any."

Simple Simon went to look
    If plums grew on a thistle;
He pricked his fingers very much,
    Which made poor Simon whistle.

He went to catch a dickey-bird,
    And thought he could not fail,
Because he'd got a little salt
    To put upon its tail.

Simple Simon went a-fishing
    For to catch a whale;
All the water he had got,
    Was in his mother's pail.

I saw a ship a-sailing,
  A-sailing on the sea,
And oh but it was laden
  With pretty things for me.

There were comfits in the cabin,
  And sweetmeats in the hold;
The sails were made of silk,
  And the masts were all of gold.

The four-and-twenty sailors,
  That stood between the decks,
Were four-and-twenty white mice
  With chains about their necks.

The captain was a duck
  With a jacket on his back,
And when the ship began to move
  The captain said Quack! Quack!

Yankee Doodle came to town,
  Riding on a pony;
He stuck a feather in his cap
  And called it macaroni.

Merry are the bells and merry would they ring,
Merry was myself, and merry could I sing;
With a merry ding-dong, happy, gay, and free,
And a merry sing-song, happy let us be!

Waddle goes your gait, and hollow are your hose,
Noddle goes your pate, and purple is your nose;
Merry is your sing-song, happy, gay, and free,
With a merry ding-dong, happy let us be!

Merry have we met, and merry have we been,
Merry let us part, and merry meet again;
With our merry sing-song, happy, gay, and free,
And a merry ding-dong, happy let us be!

I'll tell you a story
About Jack a Nory,
And now my story's begun;
I'll tell you another
About Jack and his brother,
And now my story is done.

Handy dandy, riddledy ro,
Which hand will you have, high or low?

There were three jovial Welshmen,
  As I have heard men say,
And they would go a-hunting
  Upon St. David's Day.

All the day they hunted
  And nothing could they find,
But a ship a-sailing,
  A-sailing with the wind.

One said it was a ship,
  The other he said, Nay;
The third said it was a house,
  With the chimney blown away.

And all the night they hunted
  And nothing could they find,
But the moon a-gliding,
  A-gliding with the wind.

One said it was the moon,
  The other he said, Nay;
The third said it was a cheese
  And half of it cut away.

And all the day they hunted
  And nothing could they find,
But a hedgehog in a bramble bush,
  And that they left behind.

The first said it was a hedgehog.
  The second he said, Nay;
The third said it was a pincushion,
  And the pins stuck in wrong way.

And all the night they hunted
  And nothing could they find,
But a hare in a turnip field,
  And that they left behind.

The first said it was a hare,
  The second he said, Nay;
The third said it was a calf,
  And the cow had run away.

    And all the day they hunted
      And nothing could they find,
    But an owl in a holly tree,
      And that they left behind.

One said it was an owl,
  The other he said, Nay;
The third said 'twas an old man,
  And his beard growing grey.

The Queen of Hearts
She made some tarts,
All on a summer's day;
The Knave of Hearts
He stole the tarts,
And took them clean away.

The King of Hearts
Called for the tarts,
And beat the knave full sore;
The Knave of Hearts
Brought back the tarts,
And vowed he'd steal no more.

123

Thirty white horses upon a red hill,
Now they tramp, now they champ,
    now they stand still.

] *Teeth and gums*

Robin and Richard were two pretty men,
They lay in bed till the clock struck ten
Then up starts Robin and looks at the sky,
Oh, brother Richard; the sun's very high.
You go before with the bottle and bag,
And I will come after on little Jack Nag.

"What do they call you?"
"Patchy Dolly."
"Where were you born?"
"In the cow's horn."
"Where were you bred?"
"In the cow's head."
"Where will you die?"
"In the cow's eye."

Taffy was a Welshman,
    Taffy was a thief;
Taffy came to my house,
    And stole a piece of beef.

    I went to Taffy's house,
        Taffy wasn't home;
    Taffy came to my house,
        And stole a mutton bone.

        I went to Taffy's house,
            Taffy was not in:
        Taffy came to my house,
            And stole a silver pin.

I went to Taffy's house,
    Taffy was in bed;
I took up a poker
    And flung it at his head.

125

A frog he would a-wooing go,
   Heigh ho! says Rowley,
A frog he would a-wooing go,
Whether his mother would let him or no.
   With a rowley, powley, gammon and spinach,
   Heigh ho! says Anthony Rowley.

    So off he set with his opera hat,
      Heigh ho! says Rowley,
    So off he set with his opera hat,
    And on the road he met with a rat.
      With a rowley, powley, gammon and spinach,
      Heigh ho! says Anthony Rowley.

       "Pray, Mister Rat, will you go with me?"
         Heigh ho! says Rowley,
       "Kind Mrs. Mousey for to see?"
         With a rowley, powley, gammon and spinach,
         Heigh ho! says Anthony Rowley.

          They came to the door of Mousey's hall,
            Heigh ho! says Rowley,
          They gave a loud knock, and they gave a loud call.
            With a rowley, powley, gammon and spinach,
            Heigh ho! says Anthony Rowley.

"Pray, Mrs. Mouse, are you within?"
  Heigh ho! says Rowley,
"Oh yes, kind sirs, I'm sitting to spin."
  With a rowley, powley, gammon and spinach,
  Heigh ho! says Anthony Rowley.

"Pray, Mrs. Mouse, will you give us some beer?"
  Heigh ho! says Rowley,
"For Froggy and I are fond of good cheer."
  With a rowley, powley, gammon and spinach,
  Heigh ho! says Anthony Rowley.

"Pray, Mr. Frog, will you give us a song?"
  Heigh ho! says Rowley,
"Let it be something that's not very long."
  With a rowley, powley, gammon and spinach,
  Heigh ho! says Anthony Rowley.

"Indeed, Mrs. Mouse," replied Mr. Frog,
  Heigh ho! says Rowley,
"A cold has made me as hoarse as a dog."
  With a rowley, powley, gammon and spinach,
  Heigh ho! says Anthony Rowley.

"Since you have a cold, Mr. Frog," Mousey said,
  Heigh ho! says Rowley,
"I'll sing you a song that I have just made."
  With a rowley, powley, gammon and spinach,
  Heigh ho! says Anthony Rowley.

But while they were all a-merry-making,
    Heigh ho! says Rowley,
A cat and her kittens came tumbling in.
    With a rowley, powley, gammon and spinach,
    Heigh ho, says Anthony Rowley.

       The cat she seized the rat by the crown,
           Heigh ho! says Rowley,
       The kittens they pulled the little mouse down.
           With a rowley, powley, gammon and spinach,
           Heigh ho! says Anthony Rowley.

This put Mr. Frog in a terrible fright,
    Heigh ho! says Rowley,
He took up his hat and he wished them good-night.
    With a rowley, powley, gammon and spinach,
    Heigh ho! says Anthony Rowley.

       But as Froggy was crossing over a brook,
           Heigh ho! says Rowley,
       A lily-white duck came and gobbled him up.
           With a rowley, powley, gammon and spinach,
           Heigh ho! says Anthony Rowley.

       So there was an end of one, two, three,
           Heigh ho! says Rowley,
       The rat, the mouse, and the little frog-ee.
           With a rowley, powley, gammon and spinach,
           Heigh ho! says Anthony Rowley.

I had a little pony,
   His name was Dapple Gray;
I lent him to a lady
   To ride a mile away.

     She whipped him, she slashed him,
      She rode him through the mire;
     I would not lend my pony now,
      For all the lady's hire.

The cock doth crow
To let you know:
If you be wise
'Tis time to rise.

Thirty days hath September,
April, June, and November;
All the rest have thirty-one,
Excepting February alone,
And that has twenty-eight days clear
And twenty-nine in each leap year.

See-saw, sacradown,
Which is the way to London town?
One foot up and the other foot down,
That is the way to London town.

This is the key of the kingdom;
In that kingdom there is a city;
In that city there is a town;
In that town there is a street;
In that street there is a lane;
In that lane there is a house;
In that house there is a room;
In that room there is a bed;
On that bed there is a basket;
In that basket there are some flowers.

Flowers in the basket,
Basket in the bed,
Bed in the room,
Room in the house,
House in the yard,
Yard in the lane,
Lane in the street,
Street in the town,
Town in the city,
City in the kingdom.

Old woman, old woman, shall we go a-shearing?
Speak a little louder, sir, I'm very thick of hearing.
Old woman, old woman, shall I love you dearly?
Thank you, very kindly, sir, I hear you very clearly.

131

January brings the snow,
Makes our feet and fingers glow.

February brings the rain
Thaws the frozen lake again.

March brings breezes loud and shrill,
Stirs the dancing daffodil.

April brings the primrose sweet,
Scatters daisies at our feet.

May brings flocks of pretty lambs,
Skipping by their fleecy dams.

June brings tulips, lilies, roses,
Fills the children's hands with posies.

Hot July brings cooling showers,
Apricots and gillyflowers.

August brings the sheaves of corn,
Then the harvest home is borne.

Clear September brings blue skies,
Goldenrod, and apple pies.

Fresh October brings the pheasant,
Then to gather nuts is pleasant.

Dull November brings the blast,
Makes the leaves go whirling fast.

Chill December brings the sleet,
Blazing fire and Christmas treat.

Three young rats with black felt hats,
Three young ducks with white straw flats,
Three young dogs with curling tails,
Three young cats with demi-veils,

Went out to walk with two young pigs
In satin vests and sorrel wigs.
But suddenly it chanced to rain
And so they all went home again.

In marble halls as white as milk,
Lined with a skin as soft as silk,
Within a fountain crystal-clear,
A golden apple doth appear.
No doors there are to this stronghold,
Yet thieves break in and steal the gold.

]*An egg*

Lucy Locket lost her pocket,
Kitty Fisher found it;
Not a penny was there in it,
Only ribbon round it.

The hart he loves the high wood,
    The hare she loves the hill;
The knight he loves his bright sword,
    The lady loves her will.

Cross-patch,
Draw the latch,
Sit by the fire and spin;
Take a cup,
And drink it up,
Then call your neighbors in.

Blow, wind, blow! and go, mill, go!
That the miller may grind his corn;
    That the baker may take it,
    And into rolls make it,
And bring us some hot in the morn.

Old King Cole
Was a merry old soul,
And a merry old soul was he;
He called for his pipe,
And he called for his bowl,
And he called for his fiddlers three.

Every fiddler, he had a fiddle,
And a very fine fiddle had he;
Twee tweedle dee, tweedle dee, went the fiddlers.
Oh, there's none so rare
As can compare
With King Cole and his fiddlers three.

Rich man,
 Poor man,
Beggar-man,
 Thief,
Doctor,
 Lawyer,
Indian (or merchant) chief.

There was a little guinea-pig,
Who, being little, was not big;
He always walked upon his feet,
And never fasted when he eat.

When from a place he ran away,
He never at that place did stay;
And while he ran, as I am told,
He ne'er stood still for young or old.

He often squeaked and sometimes vi'lent,
And when he squeaked he ne'er was silent;
Though ne'er instructed by a cat,
He knew a mouse was not a rat.

One day, as I am certified,
He took a whim and fairly died;
And as I'm told by men of sense,
He never has been living since.

For want of a nail, the shoe was lost,
For want of a shoe, the horse was lost,
For want of a horse, the rider was lost,
For want of a rider, the battle was lost,
For want of a battle, the kingdom was lost,
And all for the want of a horseshoe nail.

Doctor Faustus was a good man,
He whipped his scholars now and then;
When he whipped them he made them dance,
Out of Scotland into France,
Out of France into Spain,
And then he whipped them back again!

137

Little Tommy Tucker,
  Sings for his supper:
What shall we give him?
  White bread and butter.

    How shall he cut it
      Without e'er a knife?
    How will he be married
      Without e'er a wife?

        A diller, a dollar,
        A ten o'clock scholar,
        What makes you come so soon?
        You used to come at ten o'clock,
        But now you come at noon.

I married my wife by the light of the moon,
A tidy housewife, a tidy one;
She never gets up until it is noon,
And I hope she'll prove a tidy one.

    And when she gets up, she is slovenly laced,
    A tidy housewife, a tidy one;
    She takes up the poker to roll out the paste,
    And I hope she'll prove a tidy one.

        She churns her butter in a boot,
        A tidy housewife, a tidy one;
        And instead of a churn-staff she puts in her foot,
        And I hope she'll prove a tidy one.

            She lays her cheese on the scullery shelf,
            A tidy housewife, a tidy one;
            And she never turns it till it turns itself,
            And I hope she'll prove a tidy one.

Cobbler, cobbler, mend my shoe,
Yes, good master, that I'll do;
Here's my awl and wax and thread,
And now your shoe is quite mended.

The man in the moon,
    Came tumbling down,
And asked his way to Norwich;
    He went by the south,
    And burnt his mouth
With supping cold pease-porridge.

There was a man in our town
And he was wondrous wise,
He jumped into a bramble bush
And scratched out both his eyes.
And when he saw his eyes were out
With all his might and main
He jumped into another bush
And scratched them in again.

Christmas is coming, the geese are getting fat,
Please to put a penny in the old man's hat;
If you haven't got a penny, a ha'penny will do,
If you haven't got a ha'penny, God bless you.

Who killed Cock Robin?
"I," said the Sparrow,
"With my bow and arrow,
I killed Cock Robin."

Who saw him die?
"I," said the Fly,
"With my little eye,
I saw him die."

Who caught his blood?
"I," said the Fish,
"With my little dish,
I caught his blood."

Who'll make the shroud?
"I," said the Beetle,
"With my thread and needle,
I'll make the shroud."

Who'll dig his grave?
"I," said the Owl,
"With my pick and shovel,
I'll dig his grave."

Who'll be the parson?
"I," said the Rook,
"With my little book,
I'll be the parson."

Who'll be the clerk?
"I," said the Lark,
"If it's not in the dark,
I'll be the clerk."

Who'll carry the link?
"I," said the Linnet,
"I'll fetch it in a minute,
I'll carry the link."

Who'll be chief mourner?
"I," said the Dove,
"I'll mourn for my love,
I'll be chief mourner."

Who'll carry the coffin?
"I," said the Kite,
"If it's not through the night,
I'll carry the coffin."

Who'll bear the pall?
"We," said the Wren,
"Both the cock and the hen,
We'll bear the pall."

Who'll sing a psalm?
"I," said the Thrush,
As she sat on a bush,
"I'll sing a psalm."

Who'll toll the bell?
"I," said the Bull,
"Because I can pull,
I'll toll the bell."

All the birds of the air
Fell a-sighing and a-sobbing,
When they heard the bell toll
For poor Cock Robin.

Little Bob Snooks was fond of his books,
   And loved by his usher and master;
But naughty Jack Spry, he got a black eye,
   And carries his nose in a plaster.

Intery, mintery, cutery, corn,
Apple seed and briar thorn;
Wire, briar, limber lock,
Five geese in a flock,
Sit and sing by a spring,
O-U-T, and in again.

Draw a pail of water
For my lady's daughter;
My father's a king, and my mother's a queen,
My two little sisters are dressed in green;
Stamping grass and parsley,
Marigold leaves and daisies.
One with a rush! Two with a rush!
Pray thee, fine lady, come under my bush.

Sieve my lady's oatmeal,
Grind my lady's flour;
Put it in a chestnut,
Let it stand an hour.
One with a rush!
Two with a rush!
Pray thee, fine lady, come under my bush.

Georgie Porgie, pudding and pie,
Kissed the girls and made them cry;
When the boys came out to play,
Georgie Porgie ran away.

Burnie bee, burnie bee,
Tell me when your wedding be?
If it be to-morrow day,
Take your wings and fly away.

There was a bee
   Sat on a wall;
He said he could hum,
   And that was all.

Hot cross buns!
Hot cross buns!
One a penny, two a penny,
Hot cross buns!

If you have no daughters
Give them to your sons;
One a penny, two a penny,
Hot cross buns!

There was a monkey climbed up a tree,
When he fell down, then down fell he.

There was a crow sat on a stone,
When he was gone, then there was none.

There was an old wife did eat an apple,
When she had ate two, she had ate a couple.

There was a horse going to the mill,
When he went on, he stood not still.

There was a butcher cut his thumb,
When it did bleed, then blood did come.

There was a lackey ran a race,
When he ran fast, he ran apace.

There was a cobbler clouting shoon,
When they were mended, they were done.

There was a chandler making candle,
When he them stripped, he did them handle.

There was a navy went into Spain,
When it returned, it came again

I'll sing you a song,
Though not very long,
Yet I think it as pretty as any;

Put your hand in your purse,
You'll never be worse,
And give the poor singer a penny.

There was an old man,
And he had a calf,
And that's half;

He took him out of the stall,
And put him on the wall,
And that's all.

A carrion crow sat on an oak,
Fol de riddle, lol de riddle, hi ding do,
Watching a tailor shape his coat;
Sing he, sing ho, the old carrion crow,
Fol de riddle, lol de riddle, hi ding do!

Wife, bring me my old bent bow,
Fol de riddle, lol de riddle, hi ding do,
That I may shoot yon carrion crow;
Sing he, sing ho, the old carrion crow,
Fol de riddle, lol de riddle, hi ding do!

An old woman was sweeping her house, and she found a little crooked sixpence. "What," said she, "shall I do with this little sixpence? I will go to market, and buy a little pig."

As she was coming home, she came to a stile; but the pig would not go over the stile.

She went a little farther, and she met a dog.
So she said to the dog—
 "Dog, dog, bite pig!
  Pig won't get over the stile,
  And I shan't get home to-night."
But the dog would not.

    She went a little farther, and she met a stick.
   So she said—
     "Stick, stick, beat dog!
      Dog won't bite pig;
      Pig won't get over the stile,
      And I shan't get home to-night."
   But the stick would not.

She went a little farther, and she met a fire.
So she said—
 "Fire, fire, burn stick!
  Stick won't beat dog;
  Dog won't bite pig;
  Pig won't get over the stile,
  And I shan't get home to-night."
But the fire would not.

  She went a little farther, and she met some water.
 So she said—
  "Water, water, quench fire!
   Fire won't burn stick;
   Stick won't beat dog;
   Dog won't bite pig;
   Pig won't get over the stile,
   And I shan't get home to-night."
 But the water would not.

She went a little farther, and she met an ox. So she said—

"Ox, ox, drink water!
Water won't quench fire;
Fire won't burn stick;
Stick won't beat dog;
Dog won't bite pig;
Pig won't get over the stile,
And I shan't get home to-night."

But the ox would not.

She went a little farther, and she met a butcher. So she said—

"Butcher, butcher, kill ox!
Ox won't drink water;
Water won't quench fire;
Fire won't burn stick;
Stick won't beat dog;
Dog won't bite pig;
Pig won't get over the stile,
And I shan't get home to-night."

But the butcher would not.

She went a little farther, and she met a rope. So she said—

"Rope, rope, hang butcher!
Butcher won't kill ox;
Ox won't drink water;
Water won't quench fire;
Fire won't burn stick;
Stick won't beat dog;
Dog won't bite pig;
Pig won't get over the the stile,
And I shan't get home to-night."

But the rope would not.

She went a little farther, and she met a rat.
So she said—
    "Rat, rat, gnaw rope!
      Rope won't hang butcher;
      Butcher won't kill ox;
      Ox won't drink water;
      Water won't quench fire;
      Fire won't burn stick;
      Stick won't beat dog;
      Dog won't bite pig;
      Pig won't get over the stile,
      And I shan't get home to-night."
But the rat would not.

She went a little farther, and she met a cat.
So she said—
    "Cat, cat, kill rat;
    Rat won't gnaw rope;
    Rope won't hang butcher;
    Butcher won't kill ox;
    Ox won't drink water;
    Water won't quench fire;
    Fire won't burn stick;
    Stick won't beat dog;
    Dog won't bite pig;
    Pig won't get over the stile,
    And I shan't get home to-night."

The cat said, "If you will give me a saucer of
milk, I will kill the rat."
So the old woman gave the cat the milk, and when
she had lapped up the milk—
              The cat began to kill the rat;
              The rat began to gnaw the rope;
              The rope began to hang the butcher;
              The butcher began to kill the ox;
              The ox began to drink the water;
              The water began to quench the fire:
              The fire began to burn the stick;
              The stick began to beat the dog;
              The dog began to bite the pig;
              The pig jumped over the stile,
And so the old woman got home that night. 153

Theophilus Thistle, the successful thistle sifter,
In sifting a sieve full of unsifted thistles,
Thrust three thousand thistles through the thick of his thumb.
If Theophilus Thistle, the successful thistle sifter,
Can thrust three thousand thistles through the thick of his thumb,
See thou, in sifting a sieve full of unsifted thistles,
Thrust not three thousand thistles through the thick of thy thumb.

I won't be my father's Jack,
I won't be my father's Jill,
I will be the fiddler's wife,
And have music when I will.
T'other little tune,
T'other little tune,
Prithee, love, play me
T'other little tune.

One to make ready,
And two to prepare;
Good luck to the rider,
And away goes the mare.

One for the money,
And two for the show,
Three to make ready,
And four to go.

One, two, three, four, five, six, seven,
All good children go to Heaven.
Penny on the water,
Twopence on the sea,
Threepence on the railway,
Out goes she.

Bat, bat, come under my hat,
And I'll give you a slice of bacon;
And when I bake, I'll give you a cake,
If I am not mistaken.

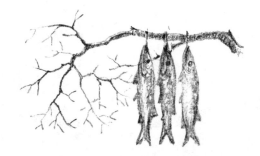

A man in the wilderness asked me,
How many strawberries grow in the sea?
I answered him, as I thought good,
As many as red herrings grow in the wood.   155

There were two blackbirds
 Sat upon a hill,
The one was nam'd Jack,
 The other nam'd Jill;
Fly away Jack,
 Fly away Jill,
Come again Jack,
 Come again Jill.

A riddle, a riddle, as I suppose,
A hundred eyes, and never a nose.
   ]*A potato*

Black within and red without;
Four corners round about.
   ]*A chimney*

A hill full, a hole full,
Yet you cannot catch a bowl full.
   ]*Mist*

Cushy cow, bonny, let down thy milk,
And I will give thee a gown of silk;
A gown of silk and a silver tee,
If thou wilt let down thy milk to me.

Old Mother Goose
  When she wanted to wander,
Would ride through the air
  On a very fine gander.

Mother Goose had a house,
  'Twas built in a wood,
An owl at the door
  For a porter stood.

She had a son Jack,
  A plain-looking lad,
He was not very good,
  Nor yet very bad.

She sent him to market,
  A live goose he bought;
"Here! mother," says he,
  "It will not go for nought."

Jack's goose and her gander
  Grew very fond;
They'd both eat together,
  Or swim in one pond.

Jack found one morning,
  As I have been told,
His goose had laid him
  An egg of pure gold.

Jack rode to his mother,
  The news for to tell.
She called him a good boy,
  And said it was well.

Jack sold his gold egg
  To a rascally knave.
Not half of its value
  To poor Jack he gave.

Then Jack went courting
  A lady so gay,
As fair as a lily,
  And sweet as the May.

The knave and the squire
  Came up at his back,
And began to belabor
  The sides of poor Jack.

But Old Mother Goose
  That instant came in,
And turned her son Jack
  Into famed Harlequin.

She then with her wand
  Touched the lady so fine,
And turned her at once
  Into sweet Columbine.

The gold egg in the sea
  Was thrown away then—
When Jack he jumped in
  And got it again.

And Old Mother Goose
  The goose saddled soon,
And, mounting his back,
  Flew up to the moon.

A was an apple-pie;
B bit it,
C cut it,
D dealt it,
E eat it,
F fought for it,
G got it,
H had it,
I inspected it,
J jumped for it,
K kept it,
L longed for it,
M mourned for it,
N nodded at it,
O opened it,
P peeped in it,
Q quartered it,
R ran for it,
S stole it,
T took it,
U upset it,
V viewed it,
W wanted it,
X, Y, Z and ampersand
All wished for a piece in hand.

Little Robin Redbreast sat upon a tree,
Up went pussy cat, and down went he;
Down came pussy, and away Robin ran;
Says little Robin Redbreast, "Catch me if you can."

Little Robin Redbreast jumped upon a wall,
Pussy cat jumped after him, and almost got a fall;
Little Robin chirped and sang, and what did pussy say?
Pussy cat said, "Mew," and Robin jumped away.

Matthew, Mark, Luke and John,
Bless the bed that I lie on.
    Four corners to my bed,
    Four angels round my head;
    One to watch and one to pray
    And two to bear my soul away.

Say in one breath:
My father he left me, just as he was able,
One bowl, one bottle, one table,
Two bowls, two bottles, two tables,
Three bowls, three bottles, three tables ...

Come, butter, come,
Come, butter, come.
Peter stands at the gate
Waiting for a butter cake.
Come, butter, come.   161

I saw three ships come sailing by,
On New Year's Day in the morning.

　　And what do you think was in them then,
　　Was in them then, was in them then?
　　And what do you think was in them then,
　　On New Year's Day in the morning?

　　　Three pretty girls were in them then,
　　　Were in them then, were in them then;
　　　Three pretty girls were in them then,
　　　On New Year's Day in the morning.

And one could whistle, and one could sing,
And one could play on the violin—
Such joy there was at my wedding,
On New Year's Day in the morning.

Jerry Hall,
He is so small,
A rat could eat him,
Hat and all.

They that wash on Monday
Have all the week to dry;
They that wash on Tuesday
Are not so much awry;
They that wash on Wednesday
Are not so much to blame;
They that wash on Thursday
Wash for shame;
They that wash on Friday
Wash in need;
And they that wash on Saturday,
Oh! they're sluts indeed.

There was an owl lived in an oak,
Whisky, whaskey, weedle;
And all the words he ever spoke
Were fiddle, faddle, feedle.

A sportsman chanced to come that way,
Whisky, whaskey, weedle;
Says he, "I'll shoot you, silly bird,
So fiddle, faddle, feedle!"

There was an old woman
Sold puddings and pies;
She went to the mill
And dust blew in her eyes.

She has hot pies
And cold pies to sell;
Wherever she goes
You may follow her by the smell.   163

I went up one pair of stairs.
    Just like me.
I went up two pairs of stairs.
    Just like me.
I went into a room.
    Just like me.
I looked out of a window.
    Just like me.
And there I saw a monkey.
    Just like me.

There was a girl in our town,
Silk an' satin was her gown,
Silk an' satin, gold an' velvet,
Guess her name—three times
    I've tell'd it.

                    ] Ann

Rub-a-dub-dub,
Three men in a tub;
And who do you think they be?
The butcher, the baker,
The candlestick-maker;
They all jumped out of a rotten potato,
164   Turn 'em out, knaves all three!

Hey diddle diddle,
The cat and the fiddle,
The cow jumped over the moon.

The little dog laughed
To see such sport,
And the dish ran away with the spoon.

Little Robin Redbreast
    Sat upon a rail;
Niddle noddle went his head,
    Wiggle waggle went his tail.

A man of words and not of deeds,
Is like a garden full of weeds;
And when the weeds begin to grow,
It's like a garden full of snow;
And when the snow begins to fall,
It's like a bird upon the wall;
And when the bird away does fly,
It's like an eagle in the sky;
And when the sky begins to roar,
It's like a lion at the door;
And when the door begins to crack,
It's like a stick across your back;
And when your back begins to smart,
It's like a penknife in your heart;
And when your heart begins to bleed,
You're dead, and dead, and dead indeed.

Sing a song of sixpence,
    A pocket full of rye;
Four and twenty blackbirds
    Baked in a pie.

When the pie was opened.
    The birds began to sing;
Was not that a dainty dish
    To set before the king?

The king was in his counting-house
    Counting out his money;
The queen was in the parlour
    Eating bread and honey.

The maid was in the garden
    Hanging out the clothes,
Along came a blackbird
    And nipped off her nose.

I love little pussy,
   Her coat is so warm,
And if I don't hurt her,
   She'll do me no harm.
So I'll not pull her tail,
   Nor drive her away,
But pussy and I
   Very gently will play.

If Candlemas Day be fair and bright,
Winter will have another flight;
If on Candlemas Day it be shower and rain,
Winter is gone, and will not come again.

Robin the Bobbin, the big-bellied Ben,
He ate more meat than fourscore men;
He ate a cow, he ate a calf,
He ate a butcher and a half,
He ate a church, he ate a steeple,
He ate the priest and all the people!
    A cow and a calf,
    An ox and a half,
    A church and a steeple,
    And all the good people,
And yet he complained that his stomach wasn't full.

Higher than a house, higher than a tree.
Oh, whatever can that be?

       ]*A star*

If you love me as I love you,
No knife shall cut our love in two!

Eggs, butter, bread,
Stick, stock, stone dead!
Stick him up, stick him down,
Stick him in the old man's crown!

Upon my word and honour
As I went to Bonner,
I met a pig
Without a wig,
Upon my word and honour.

169

As I was going up Pippen Hill,
   Pippen Hill was dirty.
There I met a pretty miss
   And she dropt me a curtsey.

There was a fat man of Bombay,
Who was smoking one sunshiny day,
When a bird called a Snipe flew away with his pipe,
Which vexed the fat man of Bombay.

Little Tee Wee,
He went to sea,
In an open boat;
And while afloat
The little boat bended,
And my story's ended.

A thatcher of Thatchwood went to Thatchet a-thatching;
Did a thatcher of Thatchwood go to Thatchet a-thatching?
If a thatcher of Thatchwood went to Thatchet a-thatching,
Where's the thatching the thatcher of Thatchwood has thatched?

There was an old woman in Surrey,
Who was morn, noon, and night in a hurry;
Called her husband a fool,
Drove the children to school,
The worrying old woman of Surrey.

"Is John Smith within?"
"Yes, that he is."
"Can he set a shoe?"
"Aye, marry, two.
Here a nail, there a nail,
Tick, tack, too."

There were two birds sat on a stone,
Fal la, la la lal de,
One flew away, and then there was one,
Fal la, la la lal de,
The other flew after, and then there was none,
Fal la, la la lal de,
And so the poor stone was left all alone,
Fal la, la la lal de.

Johnny shall have a new bonnet,
And Johnny shall go to the fair,
And Johnny shall have a new ribbon
To tie up his bonny brown hair.

And why may not I love Johnny?
And why may not Johnny love me?
And why may not I love Johnny,
As well as another body?

And here is a leg for a stocking,
And here is a leg for a shoe,
And here is a kiss for his daddy,
And two for his mammy, I trow.

And why may not I love Johnny?
And why may not Johnny love me?
And why may not I love Johnny,
As well as another body?

Eency weency spider climbed the water spout,
Down came the rain and washed the spider out,
Out came the sun and dried up all the rain,
Now eency weency spider went up the spout again.

My maid Mary
She minds her dairy,
While I go a-hoeing and mowing each morn;
Merrily run the reel,
And the little spinning-wheel,
Whilst I am singing and mowing my corn.

Onery, twoery,
Ziccary zan
Hollow bone, crack-a-bone,
Ninery, ten,
Spitt, spot,
It must be done,
Twiddlum, twaddlum,
Twenty-one.

Purple, yellow, red and green,
The King cannot reach it nor the Queen;
Nor can old Noll, whose power's so great:
Tell me this riddle while I count eight.

Jenny was so mad
She didn't know what to do;
She put her finger in her ear
And cracked it right in two.

Goosey, goosey, gander,
 Whither shall I wander?
Upstairs and downstairs
 And in my lady's chamber.

There I met an old man
 Who would not say his prayers.
I took him by the left leg
 And threw him down the stairs.

Swan swam over the sea,
Swim, swan, swim!
Swan swam back again,
Well swum swan!

Oh, do you know the muffin-man?
Oh, do you know his name?
Oh, do you know the muffin-man
Who lives in Drury Lane?

Oh where have you been, Billy Boy, Billy Boy,
Oh where have you been, charming Billy?
I have been to seek a wife,
She's the joy of my life,
She's a young thing and cannot leave her mother.

Can she bake a cherry pie, Billy Boy, Billy Boy,
Can she bake a cherry pie, charming Billy?
She can bake a cherry pie
Quick as the cat can wink its eye,
She's a young thing and cannot leave her mother.

How old is she, Billy Boy, Billy Boy,
How old is she, charming Billy?
Four times six and eight times seven
Forty-nine plus eleven
She's a young thing and cannot leave her mother.   175

The north wind doth blow,
And we shall have snow,
And what will poor robin do then?
  Poor thing!
He'll sit in a barn,
And keep himself warm,
And hide his head under his wing.
  Poor thing!

There was an old woman, her name it was Peg;
Her head was of wood, and she wore a cork leg.
The neighbors all pitched her into the water;
Her leg was drowned first, and her head followed after.

Robin Hood, Robin Hood,
  Is in the mickle wood!
Little John, Little John,
  He to the town is gone.

Robin Hood, Robin Hood,
  Is telling his beads,
All in the greenwood,
  Among the green weeds.

Little John, Little John,
  If he comes no more,
Robin Hood, Robin Hood,
  We shall fret full sore!

Polly put the kettle on,
Polly put the kettle on,
Polly put the kettle on,
 We'll all have tea.

  Sukey take it off again,
  Sukey take it off again,
  Sukey take it off again,
   They've all gone away.

There was a lady loved a swine:
"Honey," quoth she,
"Pig-hog, wilt thou be mine?"
"Grunt," quoth he.

  "I'll build thee a silver sty,
  Honey," quoth she,
  "And in it thou shalt lie."
  "Grunt," quoth he.

   "Pinned with a silver pin,
   Honey," quoth she,
   "That you may go out and in."
   "Grunt," quoth he.

    "Wilt thou now have me,
    Honey?" quoth she;
    "Grunt, grunt, grunt," quoth he,
    And went his way.   177

Ding dong bell
Pussy's in the well.
Who put her in?
Little Tommy Green.
Who pulled her out?
Little Johnny Stout.
What a naughty boy was that
To try to drown poor pussy cat,
Who never did him any harm,
But kiiled the mice in his father's barn.

There was a little woman,
  As I have heard tell,
She went to market
  Her eggs for to sell;
She went to market
  All on a market day,
And she fell asleep
  On the king's highway.

There came by a pedlar,
  His name was Stout,
He cut her petticoats
  All round about;
He cut her petticoats
  Up to her knees;
Which made the little woman
  To shiver and sneeze.

When this little woman
  Began to awake,
She began to shiver,
  And she began to shake;
She began to shake,
  And she began to cry,
Lawk a mercy on me,
  This is none of I!

But if this be I,
  As I do hope it be,
I have a little dog at home
  And he knows me;
If it be I,
  He'll wag his little tail,
And if it be not I
  He'll loudly bark and wail!

Home went the little woman
  All in the dark,
Up starts the little dog,
  And he began to bark;
He began to bark,
  And she began to cry,
Lawk a mercy on me,
  This is none of I!

179

Baa, baa, black sheep,
  Have you any wool?
Yes, sir, yes, sir,
  Three bags full;
One for the master,
  And one for the dame,
And one for the little boy
  Who lives down the lane.

Snail, snail,
Come out of your hole,
Or else I'll beat you
As black as coal.

Snail, snail,
Put out your horns,
I'll give you bread
And barley corns.

Bow, wow, wow,
Whose dog art thou?
Little Tom Tinker's dog,
Bow, wow, wow.

There was a naughty boy
And a naughty boy was he,
He ran away to Scotland
The country for to see.

There he found
That the ground
Was as hard,
That a yard
Was as long,
That a song
Was as merry,
That a cherry
Was as red,
That lead
Was as weighty,
That four-score
Was as eighty,
That a door
Was as wooden,
As in England.

So he stood in his shoes,
And he wondered,
He wondered.
He stood in his shoes
AND HE WONDERED.

This is the way the ladies ride
Tri, tre, tre, tree!
Tri, tre, tre, tree!
This is the way the ladies ride
Tri, tre, tre, tri-tre-tre, tree!

This is the way the gentlemen ride,
Gallop-a-trot, gallop-a-trot!
This is the way the gentlemen ride,
Gallop-a-gallop-a-trot!

This is the way the farmers ride,
Hobbledy-hoy, hobbledy-hoy!
This is the way the farmers ride,
Hobbledy-hobbledy-hoy!

Bow-wow, says the dog;
    Mew, mew, says the cat;
Grunt, grunt, goes the hog;
    And squeak goes the rat.

Tu-whu, says the owl;
    Caw, caw, says the crow;
Quack, quack, says the duck;
    And what sparrows say, you know.

So, with sparrows, and owls.
    With rats, and with dogs,
With ducks, and with crows,
    With cats, and with hogs,

A fine song I have made,
    To please you, my dear;
And if it's well sung,
    'Twill be charming to hear.

The rose is red, the violet blue,
The gillyflower sweet, and so are you.
These are the words you bade me say
For a pair of new gloves on Easter day.

Jack Sprat could eat no fat,
    His wife could eat no lean,
And so betwixt them both, you see,
    They licked the platter clean.

As I was going to sell my eggs,
I met a man with bandy legs,
Bandy legs and crooked toes,
I tripped up his heels and he fell on his nose.

A dog and a cat went out together
To see some friends just out of town,
Said the cat to the dog:
"What d'ye think of the weather?"
"I think Ma'am, the rain will come down,
But don't be alarmed, for I have an umbrella
That will shelter us both," said this amiable fellow.

At the siege of Belleisle,
I was there all the while,
All the while, all the while,
At the siege of Belleisle.

One old Oxford ox opening oysters;
Two tee-totums totally tired of trying to trot to Tadbury;
Three tall tigers tippling tenpenny tea;
Four fat friars fanning fainting flies;
Five frippy Frenchmen foolishly fishing for flies;
Six sportsmen shooting snipes;
Seven Severn salmons swallowing shrimps;
Eight Englishmen eagerly examining Europe;
Nine nimble noblemen nibbling nonpareils;
Ten tinkers tinkling upon ten tin tinder-boxes with ten tenpenny tacks;
Eleven elephants elegantly equipt;
Twelve typographical typographers typically translating types.

There was an old woman
Lived under a hill,
She put a mouse in a bag,
And sent it to the mill.
The miller did swear
By the point of his knife,
He never took toll
Of a mouse in his life.

Trip upon trenchers, and dance upon dishes,
My mother sent me for some barm, some barm;
She bid me tread lightly, and come again quickly,
For fear the young men should do me some harm.
  Yet didn't you see, yet didn't you see,
  What naughty tricks they put upon me:
    They broke my pitcher,
    And spilt the water,
    And huffed my mother,
    And chid her daughter,
  And kissed my sister instead of me.

There was an old man of Tobago,
Who lived on rice, gruel, and sago;
  Till, much to his bliss,
  His physician said this:
"To a leg, sir, of mutton you may go."

Mary had a pretty bird,
  Feathers bright and yellow;
Slender legs, upon my word,
  He was a pretty fellow.
The sweetest notes he always sang,
  Which much delighted Mary;
And near the cage she'd ever sit,
  To hear her own canary.

185

John Cook he had a little gray mare;
  Hee, haw, hum!
Her back stood up and her bones were bare;
  Hee, haw, hum!

John Cook was riding up Shooter's bank;
  Hee, haw, hum!
The mare she began to kick and to prank;
  Hee, haw, hum!

John Cook was riding up Shooter's hill;
  Hee, haw, hum!
His mare fell down, and made her will;
  Hee, haw, hum!

The bridle and saddle were laid on the shelf;
  Hee, haw, hum!
If you want any more you may sing it yourself;
  Hee, haw, hum!

"Little girl, little girl, where have you been?"
"Gathering roses to give to the Queen."
"Little girl, little girl, what gave she you?"
"She gave me a diamond as big as my shoe."

Pit, pat, well-a day!
Little Robin flew away.
Where can little Robin be?
Up in yonder cherry-tree.

Little John Jiggy Jag,
  He rode a penny nag,
And went to Wigan to woo:
  When he came to a beck,
  He fell and broke his neck,—
Johnny, how dost thou now?

  I made him a hat,
    Of my coat lap,
  And stockings of pearly blue;
    A hat and a feather,
    To keep out cold weather,
  So Johnny, how dost thou now?

Hickory, dickory, sacara down!
How many miles to Richmond town?
Turn to the left and turn to the right,
And you may get there by Saturday night.

What's the news of the day,
Good neighbour, I pray?
They say the balloon
Is gone up to the moon.

A long-tailed pig, or a short-tailed pig,
  Or a pig without e'er a tail,
A sow-pig, or a boar-pig,
  Or a pig with a curly tail.

There was a rat, for want of stairs,
Went down a rope to say his prayers.

Bryan O'Lin had no breeches to wear,
　So he bought him a sheepskin and made him a pair,
With the skinny side out and the woolly side in.
　"Ah ha, that is warm!" said Bryan O'Lin.

A man went a-hunting at Reigate,
And wished to jump over a high gate;
Says the owner, "Go round
With your gun and your hound,
For you never shall leap over my gate."

When Jack's a very good boy,
He shall have cakes and custard;
But when he does nothing but cry,
He shall have nothing but mustard.

High diddle doubt, my candle's out,
　My little maid is not at home;
Saddle my hog and bridle my dog,
　And fetch my little maid home.

INDEX

189